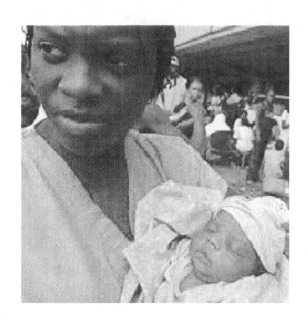

Praise For Philip Hart

"**Dr. Phil Hart is one of America's most talented and leading urban planners.** For nearly 30 years he has influenced the urban landscape from coast to coast—Boston to Los Angeles. He is an extraordinary 'thinker' and a 'doer'. Now Dr. Hart brings his years of urban planning and rebuilding to the devastated New Orleans with passion and professionalism. African Americans and the Future of New Orleans is a masterpiece—a must read for all who care about this American Treasure."
—**Jackie Jenkins-Scott**, President
Wheelock College, Boston

"Phil Hart has been a "dream maker for urban America" for years. He knows the right mix of cement and soul to create livable and economically vibrant urban communities. There is no better person to offer insight into what went wrong in New Orleans and what is right to do if the American dream is to be revived in this great American city. **African Americans and the Future of New Orleans will be recognized as a classic** not only for the precision of its insights; but also for the clarity of the challenge to our nation to "rebirth, renew, and rebuild" the crescent city."
Ambassador Charles Stith
Director of the African Presidential Archives and Research Center
Boston University

"The destruction of New Orleans by Hurricane Katrina in August, 2005, is the greatest urban catastrophe in American history. The fullest force of the extraordinary suffering this disaster caused has fallen on the shoulders of African Americans. Phil Hart tells this story with a quiet, clear and intense passion. He cuts through the stereotypes and demagoguery to give us the plain facts and, most importantly, a desperately needed clear path forward. Dr. Hart is not only a developer, planner, historian, and sociologist, he is also a passionate advocate for justice; his book is **required reading for all who care about New Orleans, the African American community and the future of urban America.**"
—John K. McIlwain
Senior Resident Fellow, ULI/J.
Ronald Terwilliger Chair for Housing

"Once again, Phil Hart focuses his sharply honed academic and analytical talents on a multi-dimensional societal disorder in critical need of a timely, effective, and efficient remedy. Once again, his incisive wisdom **offers respite from despair through the visualization of fresh, workable alternatives.**"
>
> —Fletcher H. "Flash" Wiley, Esq.,
> noted Boston attorney and business leader

"In *African Americans and The Future of New Orleans* Dr. Philip Hart **paints a compelling historical panorama of the Birth, Life and Death of New Orleans.** He effectively articulates the racial, socioeconomic and political factors that assisted Hurricane Katrina in its demise, and accentuates the importance these factors must play in the ultimate Resurrection of this true "American Dilemma.""
>
> —**Earl R. Jordan**
> Sector Leader, Ground Operations & Strategic Marketing
> West Angeles Church of God in Christ, Los Angeles, CA

"In this amazingly frank book, *African Americans and The Future of New Orleans*, Phil Hart **pulls no punches.** Even as he talks about the anguish, blame and racial divisions that still plague The Big Easy, he uses his thirty-five years of knowledge as an accomplished urban planner to help forecast how the rebirth, renewal and rebuilding of the great city of New Orleans might be accomplished."
>
> —**Vin DiBona,**
> creator and executive producer of 'America's Funniest Home
> Videos and one of Hollywood's leading television producers

"Like a skilled landscape artist, Dr. Phil Hart blends the red-tape of just talking, with the blue-print of just planning, so we can repaint the green-house of New Orleans—where every kind and color of plant can survive and flourish."
>
> —**Emmett Cooper, Ph.D.**
> Creator of the *HoneyWord Bible (For Kids of All Colors)*

Phil has shown a very powerful point of view on the City of New Orleans and its people, both before and after *Hurricane Katrina*. If you are really concerned, *African Americans and the Future of New Orleans: Rebirth, Renewal and Rebuilding—An American Dilemma* is a *MUST READ!* It has been **well crafted and carefully researched.**
>
> —Ken Hudson
> Retired Coca-Cola Executive and Former NBA Referee

African Americans and the Future of New Orleans:

Rebirth, Renewal and Rebuilding—
An American Dilemma

by Philip S. Hart, Ph.D.

African Americans and the Future of New Orleans:

Rebirth, Renewal and Rebuilding— An American Dilemma

by Philip S. Hart, Ph.D.

Amber Books
Phoenix
New York Los Angeles

African Americans and the Future of New Orleans:
Rebirth, Renewal and Rebuilding—An American Dilemma

by Philip S. Hart, Ph.D.

Published by:
Amber Books
A Division of Amber Communications Group, Inc.
1334 East Chandler Boulevard, Suite 5-D67
Phoenix, Z 85048
amberbk@aol.com
WWW.AMBERBOOKS.COM

Tony Rose, Publisher/Editorial Director   Samuel P. Peabody, Associate Publisher
Yvonne Rose, Associate Publisher/Senior Editor   The Printed Page, Interior & Cover Design
Pittershawn Palmer, Editor

Photos, maps and graphics reprinted with the permission of ULI-Urban Land Institute,
Washington, D.C.

Contents

Dedication

To the important women in my life—from my 101-year-old grand-mother Dorothy in Kansas to my mother Murlee in Colorado to my wife Tanya, daughter Ayanna and granddaughter Chloe here with me in California—I say thank you for guiding me, birthing me, loving me, supporting me, and tolerating me.

From these five generations of Harts our hearts go out to all those in New Orleans and the Gulf Coast whose lives were overturned when Hurricane Katrina blew through with all its fury leading to earth, wind and flooding. As Earth, Wind and Fire remind us, "Keep your head to the sky."

Acknowledgments

This book must acknowledge the City of New Orleans, its residents and elected officials who have seen their lives torn asunder since Hurricane Katrina blew through the Crescent City on August 29, 2005. In addition, the Urban Land Institute (ULI) must be recognized as well. I have been a ULI member for many years. Perhaps I was most proud of membership in this international land use organization when we were invited to New Orleans by the Bring New Orleans Back Commission (BNOB) to assist in developing strategies to rebuild this city after Hurricane Katrina. I think the ULI work, though controversial in some quarters, will ultimately be the blueprint which forms the new New Orleans. The ULI New Orleans advisory panel was made up of more than fifty experts in post-disaster urban redevelopment and each of these volunteers should be thanked for their dedication and resolve in this most difficult process. Of the many ULI advisory panels I have served on over the years the New Orleans panel was the most emotionally draining.

I also want to thank Amber Books Publisher Tony Rose for providing the opportunity to synthesize my experiences in urban planning and redevelopment within the context of envisioning a new New Orleans. Tony and I have been friends for many years dating back to our younger days in Roxbury, Massachusetts. I have seen Tony succeed and grow in many ways over the years, and he wears the mantle of book publisher quite well.

One of my pillars of strength during the storms associated with New Orleans, and other storms in my life, has been my church and its pastor. West Angeles Church of God in Christ and Bishop

Charles E. Blake have played important roles in my family's lives since we migrated to Los Angeles from Boston in 1990. I helped Bishop realize his dream of a West Angeles Cathedral, which was dedicated in April 2001. Bishop renewed me and my wife Tanya's vows in 1998. He christened our granddaughter Chloe in 2002. We are now together embarking on the next phase of West Angeles Church's building plans in South Los Angeles along Crenshaw Boulevard.

Finally, I must thank my wife of 39 years, Tanya Hart. We met while students at Michigan State University. I was a graduate student and she was an undergraduate student. We have been friends, companions and business partners for a long time and she has been a wise advisor in all that I do. Our daughter Ayanna Hart-Beebe has also been a strong supporter of both my wife and me. Ayanna was born in Lansing, Michigan and raised in Boston, Massachusetts. We have all been residents of Los Angeles since 1990 and I am blessed that Ayanna and my 5-year old granddaughter, Chloe, live only minutes from us in this sprawling metropolis. My mother Murlee Hart and my late father Judson Hart must also be thanked. My mother and father settled in Denver, Colorado in 1940. They met at the University of Kansas. Both my father and mother have always encouraged my two brothers and me to be the best we can be. My mother is a retired schoolteacher having taught in the Denver Public School system for over forty years. My father retired as Deputy Regional Manager of the U.S. Department of Housing and Urban Development (HUD) in Denver. He passed away in 1998 almost simultaneously with our groundbreaking ceremony for the 5,000-seat West Angeles Cathedral. As a former deacon of our family church in Denver, I know he was proud of me and my new church in Los Angeles.

All those I have acknowledged above fully prepared me for the task of visiting New Orleans in November 2005 with the ULI panel, charged with the challenge of assisting this crippled city to regain its footing. I trust this work with ULI and my book will further accelerate the rebuilding of New Orleans in a humane, inclusive and sustainable manner.

Foreword

On August 29, 2005 when Hurricane Katrina blew into New Orleans, Louisiana, the nation...indeed the world...changed. In the storm's aftermath, we saw thousands of flood victims—primarily African Americans—clinging to their lives and their life's possessions. The scene was reminiscent of a third world country.

In the storm's aftermath, people were asking the question, "God, why me?" In the face of distress that is the question we often ask God— "Why me?" But we also know that God is omnipotent and omniscient, and He knows the answer to this question. Perhaps we might want to look at a storm as Psalmist Kirk Franklin has done in one of his recent CDs. Storms bring rain, floods, destruction and despair. Storms also yield flowering gardens and can signal a rebirth. Water plays an important role in Christianity—we are reborn through the immersion in water accompanied by prayer and the healing force of redemption.

In this important book, Philip Hart examines the anguish and pain, not only of the storm's destruction of New Orleans, but also with the rebuilding of this wonderful city. Over the years, I have often preached in New Orleans, and have always found it to be a fulfilling experience. One of my closest friends, Bishop Charles Brown, lost both his home and his church in New Orleans when Katrina blew through town.

In taking us through strategies for rebuilding New Orleans, Hart has tapped into issues important to restoring many of our urban centers. In Los Angeles, my church and I have experienced earthquakes and riots that both came right to our sacred doorstep. Despite these disasters we have grown and prospered with God's guiding hand, grace and mercy.

Hart, in the sociological and urban planning context of this book, is really describing a process of healing. The church is there for healing. New Orleans needs healing—both as a city and as hundreds of thousands of individuals who have been scattered here and there—and Hart offers a prescription for healing in this important book.

I have been pleased to know Dr. Hart for nearly twenty years. We worked together to make my vision of the West Angeles Cathedral in South Los Angeles a reality. We continue to work together on our next building phases along the Crenshaw corridor. I have offered my prayers to Dr. Hart, the City of New Orleans and all those stake-holders currently involved with rebuilding New Orleans and bringing healing to the "Crescent City".

> —Bishop Charles E. Blake, Senior Pastor,
> West Angeles Church of God in Christ
> Los Angeles, California
> Presiding Bishop
> Church of God in Christ, International
> Memphis, TN
> April 2007

Introduction

I began thinking about writing this book around June of 2006. I had served on the Urban Land Institute (ULI) advisory panel assisting the Bring New Orleans Back Commission with strategies to rebuild this devastated city. We spent a week in New Orleans from November 12-18, 2005, and our report **"New Orleans, Louisiana: A Strategy for Rebuilding"** was issued in early 2006. Since August 29, 2005, when Hurricane Katrina touched down in New Orleans there have been plans, books, television documentaries, and other information put forward describing the storm and its aftermath. Blame has been spread, racial divisions exposed, class conflicts considered, people displaced, and rebuilding plans debated. Yet as of November 2006, little progress has been made in planning for the rebuilding of New Orleans.

African Americans have been a crucial component of the New Orleans landscape for over a century. Spanning their influence on music, food, culture and politics, the African American population of this great, yet declining city, has been at the center of discourse pre-Katrina and post-Katrina. I grew up in Denver, a product of a middle-class African American family. As African Americans in Denver we were always a minority population. When I finished graduate school at Michigan State University, I took my young family to Boston, Massachusetts in 1971. The African American population was a minority group in that city. So coming into a city like New Orleans where pre-Katrina the African American population was sixty seven percent was revealing. Both Denver and Boston are seen as cities on the move. New Orleans, pre-Katrina, was seen as a city on the decline. In New Orleans the rate of poverty among the African American population pre-Katrina was one in three persons. Thus, despite having a series of African American mayors since 1978, African Americans had clearly not been brought into the mainstream of the economy in the city of New Orleans. For the most part these are the folks we saw on television stranded in the Louisiana Superdome or at the Morial Convention Center after Katrina struck and the levees broke.

The city and its African American population now stand on the brink of rebirth, renewal and rebuilding. As difficult as it has been to survive Hurricane Katrina and Hurricane Rita, so too will the rebuilding process be equally arduous for different reasons. Hard decisions and difficult choices have to be made as to the footprint of the city as it rebuilds. Also unanswered is whether the population will be two-thirds African American in the new New Orleans. Also unanswered is whether the African American population can more broadly enter the mainstream of the economic life of a transformed city, or whether they will continue to be confined to the lower rungs of the social, economic and political ladder. I feel that our ability to address this question of mainstreaming outsiders is a critical component in not only the rebirth of New Orleans, but of the nation as a whole. The answer to this question remains *An American Dilemma* as sociologist and economist Gunnar Myrdal reminded us in 1944.

In 1982 New Orleans resident and retired professor of sociology at University of Massachusetts, Boston, James E. Blackwell and I provided a partial update of Myrdal's American dilemma in our book *Cities, Suburbs and Blacks: A Study of Concerns, Distrust and Alienation.* (General Hall Books, New York). In this book we surveyed the African American population in Atlanta, Boston, Cleveland, Houston and Los Angeles as to their concerns, levels of distrust, and alienation. Much of what we discussed in 1982 has relevance a quarter century later as New Orleans in its rebuilding mode grapples with distrust and alienation. Even more poignant, my friend and colleague Jim Blackwell and his lovely wife Myrt were among those forced from their homes when the levees broke.

The Blackwells had moved to New Orleans when he retired from the University of Massachusetts, Boston. Like many others, they are trying to put their lives back together after the storm.

The essence of Myrdal's groundbreaking description of an American dilemma in the mid-1940s was that the black and white populations in the United States saw the world in totally different terms. This racial divide revealed itself to Myrdal across a myriad of social, economic, cultural and political dimensions. This same racial divide has served to keep a predominantly African American city such as New Orleans from making social, economic, and political strides as it moved toward August 29, 2005. In addition, the class divide within the African American community in New Orleans added another dimension to this dilemma as the lack of mainstreaming of African American 'have-nots' continued unabated in the Crescent City.

This other dilemma of the class divide among the African American community in both New Orleans and the nation as a whole has recently been crystallized with controversial remarks made by Bill Cosby. Cosby's remarks have opened old wounds and raised questions about the responsibilities of both the African American haves and have-nots in contemporary American society. Chief among Cosby's critics have been academic Michael Eric Dyson who penned a book directed at Cosby. In turn journalist Juan Williams recently published his own book, which defends Cosby and denigrates 'poverty pimps' among established African American leadership.

These concerns in turn reveal various levels of distrust and alienation between African Americans and mainstream society, as well as between social classes within the African American community. Such concerns, distrust and alienation in concert with Hurricane Katrina produced a perfect storm of neglect, blame and inaction both pre-and-post Katrina.

The real question at this juncture is how best to give rebirth to the city of New Orleans and its citizens while renewing its spirit and zest which have enraptured a nation for so long in the process of rebuilding this crippled city and its people such that the new New Orleans can again be dubbed a city on the move.

In attempting to answer this important question the book will move through the following sections. It will begin by looking at the settlement of New Orleans in 1718 as a French colonial outpost up to its eventual growth and development and subsequent decline just as Hurricane Katrina hits the city on August 29, 2005. The next chapter will examine the pre-Katrina New Orleans, a city whose image is associated with the French Quarter and Mardi Gras—the Big Easy—which masks a disturbing reality of a declining city with a majority African American population many of whom live in below sea level neighborhoods—thus most likely to be flooded. Then comes August 29, 2005, the infamous day when Katrina blows into New Orleans with all its strength, followed by a sigh of relief, then the breaking of the levees and the breaking of a city. In this aftermath of death, despair and destruction comes the anguish, blame and racial divisions, which remain a central part of this story. Next comes the response to rebuilding, as Mayor C. Ray Nagin's Bring New Orleans Back Commission (BNOC) invites the Urban Land Institute (ULI) in to assist in drawing up strategies to rebuild this devastated city.

Chapter seven follows this process of planning for rebuilding and its subsequent stalling out as a failure to communicate engulfs all concerned parties. This failure is part of the American dilemma initially described by Swedish social scientist Gunnar Myrdal in 1944, and still perplexes us to this day. Part and parcel of this dilemma are distrust and alienation. The next chapter includes my article "Minority Developers and New Orleans" and a poem by Ed Rosenthal "Porch Talk" both reprinted from *Urban Land* magazine's October 2006 issue. This article and poem taken together capture some of this American dilemma and its attendant distrust and alien-ation. Both these sociological concepts became social truisms as the

ULI strategy for rebuilding itself became captive to the racial and social class conflicts in the post-Katrina New Orleans.

Chapter nine then posits what could be a reasonable blueprint in the rebuilding of a new New Orleans. By examining the ULI blueprint presented in November 2005 and looking at how it was misunderstood but still remains relevant, I will update this plan, its subsequent debate and action and then attempt a blueprint for rebuilding that can find sponsorship by the local, state and federal levels of government, as well as the neighborhoods which form the backbone of New Orleans.

The next three chapters then focus on Rebirth, Renewal and Rebuilding—the 3Rs of the new New Orleans. In addressing these 3Rs I will weave back and forth between social science, urban planning and development, politics, and scripture, with the goal of creating a unifying theme between rebirth, renewal and rebuilding that can be relevant to not only New Orleans, but also other cities that are grappling with issues of revitalization and redevelopment after a disaster.

Chapter thirteen describes a new New Orleans, one that is consistent with the ULI's essential elements to spur rebuilding and to ensure the city's long-term sustainability. The concluding chapter will include three of my reprinted articles from Urban Land magazine. The intent with these articles in the body of the conclusion is to provide case studies of rebirth, renewal and rebuilding after both man-made and natural disasters. Two case studies are drawn from Boston, Massachusetts that describe redevelopment after a man-made disaster in a predominantly African American section of the city. The other is drawn from Hollywood, California, a neighborhood in decline that has rebounded to reclaim its former glory in the face of an earthquake and urban riots.

—Philip S. Hart, Ph.D.

I

Settlement of New Orleans

New Orleans evolved from a small French colonial outpost surrounded by water and swamp into one of the most unique cities in America. The city was founded in 1718. What is now known as the French Quarter was laid out in a grid pattern in 1721. This downtown district now measures six blocks by thirteen blocks and is considered one of America's greatest clusters of authentic Spanish, colonial, and antebellum structures.

The story of New Orleans begins with the Vieux Carre and its traditional military site planning. However, the rest of New Orleans developed quite differently from the Vieux Carre. New Orleans grew upriver and downriver from the Vieux Carre in the early 19th century as plantations were subdivided to meet the growing population of the city. Downriver, Bernard Marigny divided his property in 1806 creating a residential extension of the Vieux Carre primarily for Creole residents, both French and African. These African Creoles were known as free men of color who at the time owned three quarters of the land in Faubourg Marigny. Upriver, land originally granted to Bienville during his term as governor in the early 1700s was subdivided as Faubourg St. Marie, later Anglicized to St. Mary by the Americans who settled there after 1803. These two new Faubourgs developed in opposite directions; St. Mary upriver with larger lots and extensive commercial and industrial development and Marigny downriver with small residential lots equal in size to those in the Vieux Carre. The city was divided into three self-governing entities, with the Vieux Carre as the First

Municipality. St. Mary became known as the American Sector and developed as the economic hub of the city.

As the Americans settled in New Orleans after 1803, other population growth came from a natural increase as well as from three major sources in the first half of the 19th century. These three sources of population growth consisted of German and Irish immigrants who came in large numbers and provided labor for various projects, including the New Basin Canal. The African population grew to twenty percent of the city as the offspring of slave owners were freed. In addition, immigrants of African descent fled the slave uprising in Haiti.

At the same time the city's elite was moving to the high ground. Esplanade Ridge became the choice location for wealthy Creole families. The avenue to this day retains its 19th century character. In the American sector wealthy families built ornate mansions up St. Charles Avenue. Many of these mansions were in the architectural style of 19th century Greek revival. In contrast to the courtyard style housing favored by the French and Spanish, the Americans preferred large front lawns or gardens, thus giving the area its current name of the Garden District.

As port activity steadily moved upriver, Magazine Street developed support services for the nearby port and was named to signify the warehouses ("magazine" in French) that lined the street for storage of tobacco and other goods awaiting export. German and Irish immigrants moved upriver to follow new jobs being created by the port. Central City became an area of immigrant settlement as it had a plentiful supply of inexpensive rental housing. Dryades Street served this neighborhood's commercial needs.

After the Civil War interrupted the city's development, a resurgence of economic and population growth occurred in the late 1800s. New Orleans became a major railroad hub, and being connected to the Port gave the city a competitive advantage in trade. The population growth during this time came from southern Europe, with large numbers of Italians, especially Sicilians, settling in New Orleans. The city was the only municipality in the South to receive substantial new immigration.

However, since much of the city was still an undrained backwater swamp, the development pressure caused by population growth was significant on the few available areas of higher ground such as Algiers Point or further along the bayou ridges and natural levees on the East Bank. Where drainage was adequate, developers could maximize the number of units constructed by building what became known as a shotgun house, and in this way responded to the housing shortage. A shotgun house is a unique style wherein the structure almost fills a rectangular lot in a linear fashion without interior hallways or closets.

In 1899 the city authorized drainage of backwater swamps using a heavy duty "Wood Pump" named after its inventor, the engineer Baldwin Wood. Using this Wood Pump large volumes of debris-laden water was raised a short vertical distance. By 1920 much of the swamp area had been drained. The majority of new residential development in the city between 1927 and 1949 occurred in the formerly backwater swamp areas known as Lakeview and Gentilly.

At the same time the city was growing into Lake Pontchartrain. In 1927 the Levee Board completed a seawall that extended 3,000 feet into the lake and added 2,000 acres of prime real estate to the city. One half of this acreage was donated to Louisiana State University (now University of New Orleans) and the other half was sold to private developers to pay off municipal bonds sold to finance the reclamation project. The resulting housing development, Lake Vista, is a carefully planned neighborhood in the "city beautiful" tradition with rear-entry cul-de-sacs and houses facing green commons.

The 1920s also saw the construction of the Industrial Canal, which was completed in 1923. The Canal determined with finality the land use pattern in the area even as it brought increased railroad activity. The Canal also isolated the Lower Ninth Ward from the rest of the city. Many Port operations shifted from the Mississippi River to the Canal, and the Canal gave the city the opportunity to centralize industrial activity and remove underutilized wharf facilities along the River without affecting the economic benefits of the Port.

The Mid-City area, especially near Earhart Boulevard and Washington Avenue, is the lowest ground in New Orleans and was the last portion of the backwater swamp to be developed. In addition to flooding, the area faced other development challenges. Property lines in New Orleans were laid our perpendicular to the River to provide all plantation owners river access, and streets followed those lines. With the River forming a crescent, streets converge in Mid-City as a hub to spokes of a wheel, forming odd-shaped lots and unusual traffic patterns.

The decades following World War II significantly changed the landscape of New Orleans. The Wagner Bill of 1937 created the United States Housing Authority, which took as its philosophy that improving the physical living conditions of the urban poor would reduce their poverty. St. Thomas, which opened in 1946, was the first public housing development in New Orleans. Like all but two of the major developments, it was built under traditional site planning concepts located at large, isolated sites with buildings clustered around open spaces used as drying yards, play areas and courtyards.

Guste Homes in Central City and Fischer Housing Development in Algiers were planned differently, each with a high-rise structure surrounded by a series of low-rise buildings and open recreational space concentrated in the perimeter. Guste Homes was built in 1964 and Fischer in1965. They were the last projects developed before the Housing Act of 1965 stipulated that public housing be scattered within the larger community rather than concentrated in major complexes.

The most dramatic changes to the city in the post-World War II years have been related to the automobile and to desegregation activities in the 1960s. With new road construction and the promise of suburban security, extensive subdivisions were built in New Orleans East and on the West Bank in the part of Algiers known as Aurora. Development on the West Bank was facilitated by the construction of the Mississippi River Bridge in the late 1950s. However, this expansion in New Orleans was exceeded by subdivision development in Jefferson Parish, so by the 1970s the city's population trend reversed course. What had been a long upward movement became a dramatic and long-term population decline, now entering its fifth decade, from over 600,000 in 1960 to 474,000 in 1997. Commerce and industry followed the population movement to the suburbs, and the oil bust of the late 1970s and 1980s affected those firms, which had remained in the city.

Construction of the high-rise interstate system facilitated this population movement and also affected the physical layout of the city. Neighborhoods have been cut in half or in some instances completely isolated. Construction of Interstate 10 destroyed the vibrant African American commercial district along North Claiborne Avenue, along with the ancient oaks that lined its neutral ground. In addition, as occurred throughout the nation, efforts by the oil industry and the automobile and bus manufacturers prompted a decision to remove the city's streetcar lines.

In the New Orleans metropolitan area, developed land increased by 47% between 1970 and 1990 even though the population rose by only eight percent. Housing construction outside the older developed parts of town exceeded growth in the number of households by seventy seven percent. As a result, not only did many older neighborhoods with historic structures enter into a long period of decline, but also property values in the region actually stagnated, even factoring in new construction. Meanwhile, in most other metropolitan areas throughout the country property values rose sharply.

The 1990s brought renewed prosperity to many segments of the community thanks to a surge in tourism and conventions, healthy activity at the Port, and a stable oil market.

Pre-Katrina New Orleans

The City of New Orleans covers 180 square miles of land and sits 90 miles north of the mouth of the Mississippi River. The city, which is coexistent with Orleans Parish, is situated 80 miles southeast of Baton Rouge, 350 miles east of Houston, 400 miles south of Memphis, and 475 miles southwest of Atlanta. New Orleans, shaped like a crescent (thus the nickname the Crescent City), is surrounded by water. The Mississippi River borders the south of the city. At Canal Street the River is 2,200 feet wide, 30-60 feet at the bankside and 100-180 feet at mid-stream. Lake Pontchartrain, which lies to the north connects with the Gulf of Mexico and covers an area of 621 square miles.

The entire city of New Orleans is from 5-10 feet below sea level. Generally speaking, the areas closer to the River are at the higher elevations. The lowest point in the state of Louisiana is in New Orleans, off Press Drive in Pontchartrain Park.

Taken as a whole, the development history of New Orleans in concert with its unique water-bound geography has yielded a rich list of pleasing attributes. Among these attributes, New Orleans enjoys a unique cultural heritage that exists in the diversity of economic and social circumstances. Its citizens feel a strong sense of community, and feel proud of the city's historic buildings and neighborhoods, its music, art, festivities, and its cosmopolitan tolerance of diverse lifestyles.

Despite its large geographic area, New Orleans is often referred to as a "15 minute city," and residents of each neighborhood in the city identified "easy access to everything" as a pleasing attribute. In addition, there was ample wildlife to be found in Bayou Savage and other areas in New Orleans East, and the Westbank, a fact that residents enjoy for sport, recreation, tourism, and a sense of a balanced ecosystem.

New Orleans has an especially vibrant downtown, offering several attractive venues, including the French Quarter, the Riverfront with the Convention Center, Riverwalk, Moonwalk, and Woldenberg Park, and the Arts District. New Orleans is also known as a good sports town. The Superdome is downtown and is home to the NFL New Orleans Saints. The NBA's New Orleans Hornets play at the new Arena.

New Orleans is a city of neighborhoods. These neighborhoods are vital and diverse with regard to cultural heritage and they share a strong sense of community. Many successful neighborhood revitalization initiatives were operating throughout the city. In addition, the unique architectural styles populating New Orleans' neighborhoods are an asset known the world over and its citizens exhibit an uncommon dedication to historic preservation.

There are several large parks in New Orleans—City Park, Audubon Park, the Zoo and Aquarium, and Armstrong Park, home to the Black Music Hall of Fame. In New Orleans East the Jazzland amusement park is under construction.

Finally, New Orleans is home to several institutions of higher education, including Tulane, Loyola, Xavier, University of New Orleans, Dillard, Delgado Community College, Our Lady of Holy Cross College, Baptist Seminary and Notre Dame Seminary.

Despite these positive attributes in the city, the City Planning Commission recognized in 1999 that without citywide economic improvement, revitalization of individual neighborhoods might result in nothing more than a shifting of impoverished families from one location to another. The prosperity of the 1990s had yet to reach large areas of the community or to stop population migration out of the city. As noted by the City Planning Commission, the challenge in the years to come is to build upon recent economic growth and neighborhood revitalization and spread their benefits throughout all areas of the city.

The continuing drop in population, combined with middle-class suburban flight, has left many areas of the city with a severe blighted housing problem. In addition to vacant housing, vacant commercial and industrial properties exist in many areas of the city. Vacant commercial and industrial property takes up large tracts of land in six of the city's thirteen main planning districts. The city is also predominantly low-rise and low-density as a majority of its citizens lived in one or two family houses before Hurricane Katrina.

The City of New Orleans, or Orleans Parish, included 215,091 housing units as of 2000 spread across thirteen planning districts and 73 neighborhoods. According to the 2004 American Community Survey, the housing stock in New Orleans is predominantly single-family homes. Sixty two percent of the housing units were single unit structures while thirty eight percent of the housing units were located in multi-unit structures. Almost ninety percent of the city's housing stock is over 25 years old with only eleven percent constructed between 1980 and 2000.

As of 2004, it was estimated that fifteen percent of the housing units in the city were vacant, meaning that roughly 180,000 households lived in the city. Of these, a slight majority, or fifty three percent, were occupied by renters with the remaining forty seven percent being owner occupied. The average household size was 2.5 people. Slightly more than one third of the households have lived in the city for more than fifteen years, which is similar to the average for the United States as a whole.

According to the U.S. Census, the median house value in the city of New Orleans in 2000 was $87,871 compared with the median house value in the United States of $119,600, which is thirty six percent higher than the median house value in New Orleans. Median house values rose twenty seven percent in the city from 1990 to 2000 while median house values escalated fifty three percent across the United States for the same time period.

In its excellent report *New Orleans After the Storm: Lessons from the Past, A Plan for the Future* issued in October 2005, the Brookings Institution noted: (1) over the years the city of New Orleans experienced more acute residential segregation and growing concentrations of poverty; (2) New Orleans once had economically and demographically diverse neighborhoods, but this pattern started to change by 1950 when some all-white neighborhoods began to form but it was not until the 1960s and 1970s that New Orleans and other Southern cities started to see the hyper-segregation of Northern cities such as Chicago and Detroit; (3) however, by the time of the storm the city of New Orleans had grown extremely segregated by both race and income; (4) racial segregation and concentrated poverty frequently coincided with each other in pre-Katrina New Orleans; (5) as a result, black and whites were living in quite literally different worlds before the storm hit.

In Gunnar Myrdal's highly influential *An American Dilemma* (1944) he identified a dual "rank order of discrimination" among the black and white population in the United States. During the time Myrdal wrote his seminal book racial prejudice, discrimination and segregation reinforced an inequality, which pervaded the institutional fabric of life in the United States (Blackwell and Hart, 1982). Myrdal's rank order of discrimination for black Americans was the exact opposite of the rank order described by white Americans. In other words, just as in Myrdal's 1944 world, so too in New Orleans before Katrina hit, blacks and whites were living in quite literally different worlds.

The nation may have moved from de jure segregation in 1944 to de facto segregation in 2005, but the results are very similar. Witness the fact that in 2000, black median household income in New Orleans was half the amount of white median household income, the black poverty rate in New Orleans was three times higher than the white poverty rate, poor blacks were five times as likely to live in areas of the city with extreme poverty rates than whites, the black college attainment rate was about four times lower than the white college attainment rate, only two-thirds of black adults had at least a high school degree compared to eighty nine percent of white adults, forty four percent of black men sixteen and older in New Orleans were not participating in the labor force compared to thirty percent for white men and forty one percent of black households own their own homes compared to fifty six percent for white households in the city. As a result, by the time Katrina stormed over the city, New Orleans had become a place sharply divided by race and class — a city where many poor black residents were geographically isolated from the rest of the population. New Orleans pre Katrina had become a microcosm of the American dilemma.

The Brookings Institution report goes on to note that simultaneously, suburban growth enabled more people and jobs to locate on newly reclaimed marshland, further isolating poor black residents in the city. Suburbanization and changing land-use patterns meant that the central city and its poor, African American residents got left behind as more and more of the population moved into new stretches of land made available through dramatic man-made changes to the physical landscape.

Thus, the predominantly African American neighborhoods that became clustered in the eastern and central portions of the city of New Orleans closely mirror the neighborhoods with high concentrations of poverty that are also clustered in the east and central portions of the city.

As with many American cities, white flight contributed to suburban growth and urban decline. In 1970, the city of New Orleans was only forty five percent African American. By 1980 the city had become a "majority minority" municipality, and by 2000 the African American share of the population had reached sixty seven percent. Driving these changes at least in part was "white flight." As large numbers of middle-class white residents left the city, low-income African American residents (though not all) tended to remain. Between 1970 and 2000, the city lost more than half of its white population but the African American population grew by twenty seven percent.

However, not all suburbanization was white. In fact, between 1970 and 2000, the African American population of all surrounding parishes grew. Almost all of black suburbanization occurred in Jefferson Parish. Jefferson Parish added almost as many African American residents as the city of New Orleans (64,000 in Jefferson, 68,000 in the city of New Orleans) representing a growth of one hundred and fifty seven percent. The result is that in Jefferson Parish, African Americans made up twelve percent of the population in 1970, but their share of the population grew to twenty three percent in 2000. These changes across the metropolitan area created a new identity for Jefferson Parish. By 2000, it was being described as an "older suburb," sharing some characteristics of central cities, e.g., aging infrastructure, growing immigrant and minority populations, and increasing poverty rates.

The shifting of population and jobs from the central city to the outlying parishes resulted in sprawling development patterns. Rather than building up density in New Orleans, the region instead found ways to build out. Density barely changed at all in the city of New Orleans between 1970 and 2003. New Orleans's historic love affair with low-rise structures continued unabated even in a region so constrained by natural barriers.

The end result is that the New Orleans metropolitan area was consuming land at a much faster clip than its population growth appeared to warrant. For example, between 1982 and 1997, the metropolitan area lost one point four percent of its population. But during this same period, the number of new square miles of urbanized land grew twenty five percent from 1982 levels. Because of the population loss coupled with the large gain in land consumption, the region actually "de-densified," meaning its density (population per acre) dropped twenty one point one percent. This drop in density was a slightly larger drop in density than in the nation, which dropped twenty point five percent.

It is important to note that much of the land that the region consumed in the post-war years was former wetlands. Engineering allowed the reclamation and development of this previously undevelopable land, but it remained vulnerable to flooding. Ultimately, a much vaster swath of the region's low-lying flood plain had been converted to subdivisions and other uses when Katrina hit than had been in 1950.

As noted in the Urban Land Institute report "New Orleans, Louisiana: A Strategy for Rebuilding" (2006), presently much of the city sits one to ten feet below sea level, and a complex system of levees, canals, floodwalls, and pumps is still necessary to remove storm water from these low-lying areas. Many of the low-lying areas inhabited after 1940 were flooded after Katrina. This pattern of flooding suggests that any recovery plan for the city needs to incorporate a more effective and integrated system of stormwater management and infrastructure that will account for the city's fundamental topography and hydrology.

The ULI report goes on to note that given the city's position in the dual network of waterways, coupled with the Gulf of Mexico's coastal erosion, that pre-Katrina, the water was already at the city's gates. Stated differently, land loss in coastal Louisiana has reached catastrophic proportions, accounting for ninety percent of the nation's total coastal marsh loss. This reality is relevant to both the pre-and-post Katrina city of New Orleans. Land loss has directly affected the city's vulnerability to large storm events. The natural protective barriers surrounding New Orleans have been lost, leaving the city at its most vulnerable since its founding in 1718. Thus, during a Category 3 hurricane, every three miles of marshland can stop up to one foot of storm surge. Before Katrina, coastal Louisiana was expected to have lost almost 1.5 million acres by 2050, according to the LCA Ecosystem Restoration Study. Current evidence suggests that east of the Mississippi River, Katrina's intensity may have already eroded the barrier islands with such force that they have been diminished to the condition projected for 2050. If this is true, erosion and land loss have reached the city proper.

The pre-Katrina New Orleans thus stood on the brink of a perfect storm. The city had developed in such a way as to make habitable swamp and marshland thus creating new neighborhoods as the surrounding water moved ever closer to the city's gate. This was all while relying on a complex system of levees and pumps that were built and managed by equally complex sets of bureaucracies. At the same time, more dense development had been frowned on in New Orleans. These events preceded Katrina hitting the city, which at the time was being governed by a city administration headed by a new mayor unschooled in how to effectively negotiate with powerful public bureaucracies on his city's behalf.

This perfect storm was mirrored at the state level with a Democratic governor, Kathleen Babineaux Blanco, who had a tense relationship with New Orleans Mayor C. Ray Nagin even before Katrina hit the Crescent City. Further compounding this perfect storm was a distracted Republican White House led by President George W. Bush, along with a majority Republican Senate and House of Representatives that seemed to have little use for formulating a coherent urban policy or for the urban poor. Compounding this sad tale is the historic New Orleans and Louisiana penchant for cronyism, patronage and political shenanigans, which rendered the city and state somewhat of a laughingstock with little clout in certain important quarters.

August 29, 2005

"According to the grace of God which was given unto me, as a wise master builder I have laid the foundation, and another builds on it. But let each one take heed how he builds on it."

—1 Corinthians 3:10

The land loss in coastal Louisiana has reached catastrophic proportions and this loss directly affected the city's vulnerability to large storm events. Thus, with this land loss and the development of much of the city on marshland and swamp over its fairly recent history, by the time Hurricane Katrina moved toward New Orleans the city was at its most vulnerable since its founding.

Besides the suspect physical foundation underlying the below sea level neighborhoods of the city, so too was the social foundation weakening. Whereas New Orleans once had economically and demographically diverse neighborhoods, this pattern started to change in 1950, when some all-white neighborhoods and all-black neighborhoods began to form. By the time of the storm, the city of New Orleans had grown extremely segregated by both race and income.

Within the context of this weakening geographical and social structure of the city, Tropical Storm Katrina shifted slightly to the east just before dawn on the morning of Monday, August 29, 2005. This

Category 4 hurricane with winds up to 145 miles per hour then roared into the central Gulf Coast just east of the city of New Orleans.

Having initially believed the worst of Hurricane Katrina had spared the city, reports then broke that floodwalls protecting New Orleans' Lower 9th Ward and running along 17th Street and London Avenue had breached, flooding vast areas of the city. With the subsequent flooding, thousands of modest homes in low-lying urban neighborhoods and others in black and white suburbs were under water. At the same time, above sea level neighborhoods such as the French Quarter and the downtown district remained dry, sustaining mainly damage from the high winds.

What unfolded was then a humanitarian crisis not seen on the American shores since the Great Depression of the 1930s. Then came the images of a botched evacuation and more than 20,000 people, mainly poor African Americans, expecting aid, but instead finding grim conditions inside the New Orleans Superdome.

Having made the trip via bus from the Lower 9th Ward while on a ULI tour in November 2005, I could only imagine what this trek must have been like for the weak, infirm, and even healthy souls in the midst of a hurricane to make such a trip by foot across the Industrial Canal to downtown New Orleans. And then, once at the Superdome, after such an arduous trek to find the squalid conditions and the need to beg for relief for the basic necessities of life. Clearly, the social foundation of the city of New Orleans was built on shifting sand.

The breach in the levees revealed that the infrastructure so critical to the survival of the city in such a storm was also built on a suspect foundation. As noted by Warren Whitlock in Urban Land magazine (January 2006), Katrina left more than 75 percent of New Orleans submerged under as much as 14 feet of water from Lake Pontchartrain and the Industrial Canal. Evidence mounts that substandard design and construction on the pre-Katrina levee system played a significant part in its demise during the storm. Further, as Whitlock notes, in the city the levees are but one of the infrastructure systems that need to be rebuilt safely and swiftly.

Thus, on Tuesday, August 30, 2005, when the levees broke, the weaknesses of both the geographical and social foundations of the city of New Orleans were laid bare for the world to see. The twin images of breached levees along with people begging for help in flooded homes and neighborhoods as well as at the Superdome spoke volumes about the sagging fortunes of the Crescent City even before Katrina blew into town. Further, as Whitlock notes, the longstanding fears of insufficient levee protection and the longstanding mistrust of local authorities complicated matters before Katrina hit and in the subsequent recovery.

Indeed, before the storm metropolitan New Orleans was a racially divided low-wage metropolis built on a marsh in hurricane country. So as events unfolded on August 29 and the days to follow, it would become abundantly clear to all that the foundation that had been laid was weak and that it would take a 'masterbuilder' equipped with a plan to address both the physical and social fabric of this city in order to put it back together again.

The images that began flooding the airwaves showed mostly poor African Americans who were unable to flee the city prior to the storm hitting with full force. They were left as in a third world country bereft of resources to fend for themselves. The nation and the world were astonished at the prevailing picture of need and neglect portrayed in those confounding days following August 29.

Myrdal's 'rank order of discrimination' became once again a relevant concept in the face of the seemingly unending tide of black and brown faces that were captured speaking to media from CNN, NBC, ABC, CBS, and other outlets as they waited impatiently for some relief. Of course, there were white faces among those seen pleading with the cameras, but the vast majority of those seen were African Americans.

Russell's Photos
By Ed Rosenthal Poet-broker

Chandeliers in trees
porches upside down
Mailbox without house

Miles of clapboard houses
coded like Israelite's huts
against the angel of death
who came back around
for a second look
and then a third
at the hieroglyphs
scrawled on boarded walls
Remove dead animal
Dead animal removed
Bloated body in basement

The boarded windows
of these squat structures
are like eyes shaded
against the glare of silence
They stare at you
the only witnesses
that life lived here

Except for the stench
of rotted flesh
that filled the photographers
Eye sockets

Steps without doors
Floating houses
Toys tangled in treetops

Piles of building bones
thrown down by Katrina
Stuck like giant sticks
In the middle of a game
Waiting for a gamblers hand
To be picked up and tossed again.

Russell Brown, an LA Artist, visited New Orleans the first Jazz Festival after Katrina. He shot hundreds of photos of Ninth Ward and Elysian Fields.

As the clouds broke and the storm passed, it then became clear that by a wide margin Hurricane Katrina would rank as the most costly natural disaster in United States history. The damage would prove to be four times that incurred by Hurricane Andrew in 1992. However, unlike Andrew, Katrina exposed a raw nerve rooted in an American dilemma, that of the wide chasm of the racial divide in this nation.

Listening to the gruesome stories from the Louisiana Superdome and the Morial Convention Center in New Orleans, in a strange way it was a weary reminder of African slaves being transported to the New Land tightly packed below deck beginning four centuries ago. Only in this instance it was New Orleans, Louisiana in the year 2005 with primarily low income African Americans who were tightly packed into the Superdome and Convention under grueling conditions.

With 25,000 people packed into the Superdome and up to 30,000 in the Convention Center after Katrina had rendered them homeless, conditions in both venues had become horrendous. There was no air conditioning, the toilets were backed up, and the stench was so bad that medical workers wore masks as they walked around.

Jeff Duncan's "Dome Series" in the New Orleans Times Picayune's five part series one year after Hurricane Katrina ran from August 27 to August 30, 2006, and provides a narrative as to the horrors in the Louisiana Superdome. Here are selected excerpts.

> *"The crowd consisted largely of African-American families. Many of them were poor. Some were sick or elderly. … . City officials did their part to warn evacuees of the conditions they'd face in the Dome. The building could be without power and water pressure for days. It would be crowded and hot. … . Conditions inside the Dome deteriorated rapidly Monday night. With no circulation, the air grew heavy. Condensation coated the walls and walkways. … . The increased population only added to the misery of the folks inside. They already were*

trying to endure the unrelenting heat and choking stench of human waste. Now they were crowded by hordes of wet, desperate people from off the streets. ... . Regina Wheat wasn't as lucky. She was stuck in the mass and mayhem on the bridge. She had survived the Dome since arriving from her eastern New Orleans home Sunday on a combination of guile and determination. ... . By Thursday, the stench of human waste inside the Dome had become unbearable. The folks inside had long stopped using the bathrooms. Instead, people improvised. ... . The crowd had more than doubled since Sunday as holdouts by the dozens arrived via helicopter, boat or truck. A population the size of New Iberia now was jammed into the Dome's labyrinthine corridors and 1.9 million square feet."

Compare this to Alex Haley's novelization of conditions on slave ships during the Middle Passage in his acclaimed *Roots* (1976) fictional account of this horror.

"Kunta wondered if he had gone mad. Naked, chained, shackled, he awoke on his back between two other men in a pitch darkness full of steamy heat and sickening stink and a nightmarish bedlam of shrieking, weeping, praying and vomiting."

In the 1990 BET documentary film "Dark Passages" I produced with my wife Tanya Hart and Valerie Whitmore-Guscott we tell the story of the Atlantic slave trade. This nonfiction film was shot on location in West Africa and provides the following transcription.

Tanya Hart: *The Middle Passage was notorious for the number of deaths that occurred. Packed like sardines on the slave ships, the death tolls averaged fifteen to twenty percent. The slaves were packed so tightly on the ship they could neither lie full length nor sit upright.*

Dr. David Blight: *By the middle of the eighteenth century a serious business argument ensued over the so-called loose packing and tight packing techniques. Simply put, the argument was if you put two hundred slaves in a ship and you gave them some space as human beings to move, would the mortality rate be such that you'd get more successfully landed in the New World, or if you put four hundred on the ship and indeed stacked them, tight packed them as it was called, would you get a greater return? Over time and experimentation with this hideous system, they found that tight packing got a greater return.*

Louis Gossett, Jr.: (In a slave narrative) *"We were taken in a boat from place to place and sold every place we stopped at. . . . The slaves we saw on board the ship were chained together by the legs below deck, so close they could not move. . . . .The place they were confined in below deck was so hot and nasty I could not bear to be in it."*

Dr. David Blight: *Well, the conditions were horrible. Vincent Harding in his book, There Is a River, uses the phrase, he calls the slave ships 'the cramped and fetid waiting rooms of history.' Eyewitness accounts abound of how you could smell a slave ship five miles downwind, if the wind was right.*

Though separated by centuries, these two sets of narratives—from slavery to freedom—bespeak the evolution from Africans forced from their homeland to the horrors of slave ships surrounded by water to African Americans forced from their homes to the horrors of a football stadium and convention center surrounded by water. We have come a long way in terms of time and space, but perhaps not as far as we would like to think in terms of true freedom.

As noted in **Urban Land** magazine in January 2006, in an edition titled *Build or Bury: Gulf Coast storms—planners' greatest challenge* with its 24-page special report "A Rude Awakening," the inability to care for those left behind after the immediate aftermath of the hurricane quickly revealed to the nation a city divided along racial lines. The racial dividing line in New Orleans that was surfaced by

Katrina and its aftermath is a microcosm of the nation. To a large extent, this racial dividing line was drawn beginning with the Atlantic slave trade, fought for in the Civil War, accentuated in the Jim Crow era, documented in a social science framework by Myrdal in 1944, codified legally by the U.S. Supreme Court in 1954 with the Brown vs. Board of Education decision, reinforced by the Kerner Commission Report in 1968 after the urban riots, colorized by the Civil Rights and Black Power movements in the 1960s and 1970s, and punctuated by Hurricane Katrina in 2005—truly a continuing rude awakening for America.

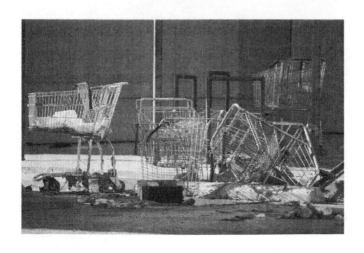

IV

Anguish, Blame and Race

The initial response to the storm was an inadequate evacuation plan by the city of New Orleans. This lack of preparedness on the local level only presaged the coming weak response from the Federal Emergency Management Administration (FEMA). This lack of coordinated and timely response on the part of the public sector at the local, state and federal levels served to cripple New Orleans significantly and place in full relief the depths of the racial and class dilemma facing the nation.

Though both white and black communities were impacted by Katrina, given that New Orleans was two-thirds African American pre-storm, it is only to be expected that the bulk of despair would fall on this racial group. It is perhaps even more ironic that a majority African American city hit by the worst natural disaster in American history would be governed by an African American mayor.

In his insightful book *Come Hell or High Water: Hurricane Katrina and the Color of Disaster (2006),* Michael Eric Dyson in the Preface raises the following questions regarding New Orleans: "Why did the black and poor get left behind? What took the government so long to get to the Gulf Coast, especially New Orleans? What do politicians sold on the idea of limited government offer to folk who need, and deserve, the government to come to their aid? Why is it that the poor of New Orleans, and, really, the poor of the nation, are hidden from us, made invisible by our disinterest in their lives?

Why was it a surprise that they are in as bad shape as the storm revealed? Does George Bush care about black people? Do well off black people care about poor black people?"

Dyson then attempts to answer these provocative questions throughout his ten-chapter book. In this chapter, I will reference key points raised by Dyson in combination with work on race and class done by New Orleans Katrina evacuee James E. Blackwell and me since 1982. The book Blackwell and I published in 1982 *Cities, Suburbs and Blacks: A Study of Concerns, Distrust and Alienation* states in its Preface, "President Reagan has set this nation on a course which will, if unchecked by the Courts, escalate racial and class enmity, terminate the bloodstained national commitment to achieve racial harmony and equality, and broaden the condition of racial apartheid that exists in so many institutions and metropolitan areas." Further, "The Reagan Administration seems unconcerned about the conditions of racial minorities and the poor."

Compare this analysis with Dyson's series of questions some quarter of a century later in the wake of Katrina when he queries, "Would Bush and the federal government have moved faster to secure the lives of the hurricane victims if they had been white? The question must be partnered with a second one that permits us to tally a few of the myriad injuries of the racial contract that has bound American citizens together: did the largely black and poor citizens of the Gulf Coast get left behind because they were black and poor?"

In 1983, Blackwell and I were commissioned to draft a working paper for The Boston Committee titled "Race Relations in Boston: Institutional Neglect, Turmoil and Change." This paper could be redrafted and titled "Race Relations in New Orleans: Institutional Neglect, Turmoil and Change." Clearly, despite being governed by Democrat African American mayors since 1978, much work remained to be done to bring the majority of New Orleans' African American population into the mainstream of the city's social, political and economic life. Thus, it is not farfetched to declare that local, state and national elected officials had neglected poor blacks, be they Democrat or Republican. Turmoil came in the form of a natural disaster on August 29, 2005 when Hurricane Katrina blew into the Crescent City. The question now is the nature of the change that will take place on the heels of the neglect and the turmoil.

In addressing this process from the standpoint of neglect, turmoil and change, I will spend some time addressing one section of the Blackwell and Hart 1983 working paper. That is, "Why Do People Discriminate?" Discrimination can be racially based or class based, or for a myriad of other social, economic, political, cultural and gender reasons.

In our working paper, Blackwell and I assert that discussions of inter-group relations invariably focus on various dimensions of attribution; that is on characteristics employed to identify and separate or categorize persons as members of a dominant or subordinate group. Universally, dominant groups are assumed to possess and control access to the important values, scarce resources and rewards of the social system. The dominant group is believed to have inordinate power and influence, as well as political and economic control. This power enables the dominant group to control decision making, to manipulate the distribution of highly prized values (e.g., jobs, money, income, wealth accumulation, education, housing, health benefits, and others), and to make determinations about the overall life-chances of all persons who come under dominant group control.

By contrast, subordinates or minority groups have limited access to the highly prized values and scarce rewards, are often regarded as either biologically or intellectually inferior or both to members of the dominant group (thus less entitled to important resources), believed to possess an inferior culture, are categorized and demeaned and subject to prejudice, discrimination and segregation.

Dominant groups may use racism, prejudice and institutional discrimination as mechanisms to assure the maintenance of power and control. Racism is more than an attitude that favors the dominant group members over the minority; it is a belief system coupled with behavior that actually results in the acquisition of a disproportionate share of important resources and a greater sense of freedom and entitlement.

Racism becomes institutional whenever the dominant group creates arrangements and solidifies practices within established social institutions designed for the benefit of that group over others. In general, attributions of dominance and subordination and ascriptions of prejudice and discrimination sometimes overlook two important facts. The first is that minorities may also be prejudiced against members of the dominant group and that minorities may also harbor demeaning stereotypes against the dominant group and toward members of other minority groups.

There is a tendency to claim that minority group prejudices against members of the majority group are reaction formations to the behavior of dominant group members toward minorities. The presumption is that were it not for dominant group prejudices there would not be a minority group response of prejudice against the superordinates. The second fact is the tendency to treat minority groups and dominant groups as essentially homogeneous entities. This denies the existence of disparate belief systems, practices, and interaction patterns within each of these groups. It also denies that some minority members indeed rank higher on any objective measure of achievement than many members of the dominant group.

Why people discriminate may be addressed in terms of structural conditions and patterns of interactions in the marketplace as well as in other forms of interpersonal relations. In more recent times, attention has focused on explanations for discrimination in the marketplace. In this situation, discrimination is explained in terms of either, exogenous theory or a "taste for discrimination", endogenous theory, economic loss, and learned behavior.

Forty years ago noted economist Lester Thurow argued that white males monopolize power; it is this monopolization that is so critical to discrimination since, without it, less racial prejudice would be directed toward racial minorities (Thurow, 1967). In examining these various theories, irrespective of how such questions are answered, one fact is indisputable. Discrimination is more likely to persist when it is supported by the culture, is or thought to be sanctioned by the leadership structure of a given community, neighborhood, institution or employer.

Concurrently, the race class issue has continued to be debated as to its importance in the matter of discrimination. Beginning with William Julius Wilson's 1978 book **The Declining Significance of Race** to Shelby Steele's **White Guilt** (2006), black scholars have put forth the premise that one's class position is now more important in determining life-chances than race. Wilson further argued that if the black 'underclass' had marketable skills, better education and training, they would not experience discrimination.

There is evidence to show that while the income levels of both African Americans and whites have increased over the past several decades, the gap between median family incomes for these two groups has widened. There is also some evidence showing that even when one controls for such factors as age, education and occupation, African Americans receive incomes considerably below that of whites. In addition, without question African Americans and other minorities do not have equal access to housing, health care and education, even as we move further into the 21st century.

One mechanism suggested in the social science literature to reduce prejudice or intergroup tension is economic improvement. Expressions of prejudice and acts of discrimination seem to parallel fluctuations in the economy. When times are good, people seem more willing to share or to be less disturbed by competition. When times are bad and competition for jobs and limited resources increases, scapegoating tends to rise.

As we consider the anguish visited upon individuals, families, neighborhoods, indeed an entire city by Hurricane Katrina, it is perhaps a bit easier to relate to the blame game that has been played out since August 29, 2005. Some place the blame on Mayor C. Ray Nagin for not fully preparing his city for the storm and the resultant evacuation, thus stranding thousands of poor, African American residents of the city in an untenable situation. Others blame President George W. Bush and FEMA for their too little, too late approach to the matter. Michael Eric Dyson feels Bush's blueblood upbringing is one explanation for his lack of concern for the largely African American city of New Orleans.

In the *New York Times* bestseller *The Covenant* (2006), Robert Bullard states in his essay on "Assuring Environmental Justice For All," that "Hurricane Katrina exposed the systematic weakness of the nation's emergency preparedness and response to disasters. The powerful storm also exposed the racial divide in the way the U.S. government responds to natural and manmade disasters in this country....Because of the enormous human suffering and environmental devastation, the rebuilding of New Orleans and the Louisiana, Mississippi, and Alabama Gulf Coast region will test the nation's ability and commitment to address lingering social inequality and institutional barriers that created and maintained the racial divide of 'two Americas,' one black and poor and the other white and affluent."

Bullard is referring to 'environmental racism,' a situation he documents by noting that: Katrina caused six major oil spills; the storm hit sixty underground storage tanks, five Superfund sites, and four hundred sixty six industrial facilities that stored highly dangerous chemicals before the storm; it created a 'toxic soup' with e. coli in the floodwaters as more than one thousand drinking-water systems were disabled; Katrina left behind an estimated 22 million tons of debris, with more than half—12 million tons—left in Orleans Parish; flooded homes containing over one million pieces of 'white goods,' such as refrigerators, stoves, and freezers, require disposal; an additional 350,000 automobiles must be drained of oil and gasoline and then recycled; more than 110,000 of New Orleans' 180,000 houses were flooded, and one-half of these sat for days or weeks in more than six feet of water; as many as 30,000 to 50,000 homes in New Orleans may have to be demolished; the storm closed the New Orleans school system and left a trail of toxic muck in classrooms and on playgrounds (over 93 percent of the city's 125,000 public school children are African American).

Spike Lee's excellent four act documentary film that aired on HBO tells the story of anguish, blame and race in a moving manner. Titled "When the Levees Broke: A Requiem in Four Acts—An American Tragedy," this stirring television telling of the Katrina story is riveting. As Spike reminds us, "Most people think that it was Katrina that brought about the devastation to New Orleans. But it was a breaching of the levees that put 80 percent of the city under water. It was not the hurricane." My wife Tanya and I screened Acts I and II at NBC Universal Studios before HBO aired the film. It was especially emotional viewing "When the Levees Broke" in a screening room with 35-40 other people, some of whom we knew well and others not so well. Having experienced the tragedy in New Orleans as a member of the Urban Land Institute (ULI) advisory services team in November 2005, it was doubly emotional to see the city and its people from such a high production value perspective as provided by Spike Lee.

Clearly, there is more than enough blame to go around. To what extent is the lack of preparedness and tardy response due to racism, classism, incompetence or indifference? Does George Bush dislike black people as suggested by Michael Eric Dyson? Does Ray Nagin hold low-income African American members of his city in such low regard that their welfare was an afterthought? To what extent is the power structure of New Orleans still primarily ruled by white males? Why is it that after over a quarter century of black mayoral control in New Orleans that the poverty rate among this racial group has not changed significantly?

New Orleans, like many other American cities, was a 'majority minority' city pre-Katrina. Two-thirds of its population was African American. Thus, from simply a numerical standpoint, the African American 'minority' was actually a 'majority.' Did this 'majority' status within the city translate into political and economic gains as the social science theory suggests should follow? Clearly, significant strides had been made in the political arena—witness the series of African American mayors since 1978, including two generations of one family with the Morials. In addition, there was substantial representation on the City Council, and other elected offices. However, as noted earlier the poverty rate among African Americans was one in three pre-Katrina. The public schools were a mess. The Mayor and City Council (with an African American President) were constantly at odds. At what point should we expect that such political gains will translate into real progress on the part of this 'majority' constituency?

As to economic dominance in New Orleans pre-Katrina, the white power structure still reigned supreme. Despite being a predominantly African American city, the economic strings were still being pulled by the 'minority' white business leaders. When Ray Nagin first won his run for mayor in May 2002, the white business community provided key support. Some dubbed Nagin a puppet of the white establishment. With his second run in 2006, Nagin was viewed more sympathetically by the African American community and won re-election based upon their support.

Within this context of discussing race and class in New Orleans, and the response to Katrina's aftermath, it is perhaps relevant to ask, is George Bush racist? Is Ray Nagin a class-conscious African

American mayor of a predominantly African American city, whose first obligation is to the middle class? To what extent will race and class conflict inhibit New Orleans from rebuilding in such a way as to move the city forward as a major American metropolis? Will the city be revived? What will the footprint of the city be in 5, 10, 20 years? Will the city be predominantly African American in 5, 10, 20 years?

Clearly there are more questions than answers as we move more than one year from the devastation visited upon New Orleans. As of this writing the most accurate estimate is that the city has around 200,000 residents. Outside of the neighborhoods above sea level, there is spotty rebuilding thus rendering something akin to a 'jack-o-lantern' effect in the low-lying neighborhoods.

What we have witnessed is a human tragedy on a large scale. Lives have been altered, partially due to human error and negligence. There has been plenty of anguish to last for the next century. There has been enough blame to spread around to the most likely targets. Race and class conflict has been exposed, with some debating whether the acts of omission and commission have primarily to do with color or class.

At this point in time, it is past time to try and put the anguish, blame and race baiting behind and turn attention fully to rebuilding a unique city that has played such a vital role in the history of this nation.

V

Strategies For Rebuilding

It is responsible to formulate a plan of action before rebuilding on such a large scale as is required in New Orleans. Mayor C. Ray Nagin was wise to begin this process by appointing a 17-member Bring New Orleans Back Commission (BNOB). Made up of business and civic leaders, this Commission was initially charged in October 2005 with coming up with strategies by the end of 2005 to rebuild the city. In setting out to accomplish this daunting task, upon the advice of prominent New Orleans real estate developer and banker, Joseph Canizaro, the international land use organization the Urban Land Institute (ULI) was asked to assemble a team of post disaster and redevelopment experts to assist the Commission in its mission.

Canizaro has a special relationship with ULI, serving as a former Chairman of this nonprofit organization headquartered in Washington, D.C., and has one of ULI's senior fellow's chairs named after him. A staunch Republican, Canizaro would prove to be a catalyst for redevelopment planning, but also a lightning rod for criticism of the ULI strategies for rebuilding New Orleans.

At the ULI Fall Meeting in Los Angeles in October 2005, the team began its work, while at the same time the ULI Foundation launched a fund drive to underwrite our work in New Orleans and the Gulf Coast. New Orleans was strapped for cash before Katrina, and was even more so after Katrina did its damage. Normally, if a municipality invites a ULI advisory services team to its community, it assumes the underwriting costs of this endeavor in the role of a sponsor. New Orleans was unable to meet this obligation, but this did not deter ULI as the Foundation proceeded to raise over $1 million from its members to underwrite this important work.

Generally ULI advisory service panel engagements run 3-5 days depending upon the scope of the assignment. Such panels are usually made up of 8-9 land use experts that have no vested interest in issues to be addressed on the assignment. For a five-day panel ULI charges the sponsor a fee of $120,000 that covers expenses while the panelists serve as volunteers. Unlike in other cities, the New Orleans panel had 50 members. ULI, as an organization, devoted much of its staff and senior fellow resources to this once-in-a-lifetime assignment to save a drowning city. In 1994, an urban planning foundation, The American City Coalition that I ran with Boston real estate developer Joseph E. Corcoran co-sponsored a panel in Roxbury, Massachusetts with the City of Boston and the Bank of Boston. In 2001 The American City Coalition co-sponsored an advisory panel visit to Hollywood, California along with the Hollywood Chamber of Commerce and the ULI Foundation. The report from this panel visit titled *A Strategy for Hollywood's Comeback* and its recommendations have helped guide the multi-billion redevelopment of perhaps the most famous neighborhood in the world.

Since 1947 when ULI's advisory services panel program was initiated, over 400 assignments have been carried out with municipalities, nonprofit organizations, universities, private sector clients, and a host of others. ULI panel visits are seen as an effective way to engage high-level land use professionals in assisting sponsors with complex redevelopment issues. If a sponsor were to hire the same 8-9 land use professionals at their normal fees for five days, the costs could run 5-10 times what a ULI advisory panel visit would charge.

As described in Jed Horne's gripping book *Breach of Faith: Hurricane Katrina and the Near Death of a Great American City:*

City council president Oliver Thomas was on the BNOB Committee, another African American, as were a variety of less well-known civic leaders. And one of the committee's first moves was to accept an offer from the Urban Land Institute, a prestigious city planning group, to come up with recommendations for the city that New Orleans needed to become in the post-Katrina world. (p. 215, 2006)

As Horne notes, there were suspicions from the start about the racial makeup of the BNOB, as well as the role of Canizaro. A prodigious fundraiser for the Republican Party, Canizaro seemed to relish reminding people of his close ties to the White House and Karl Rove, and that this special relationship would put New Orleans in good stead in terms of federal funding support for the rebuilding of the city.

Canizaro's role and the subsequent ULI recommendations regarding the footprint of the new New Orleans and its racial makeup complicated the process of putting a plan in place that could gain consensus. As Horne describes it:

But the economic argument against repopulating the entire city leaned on speculative judgments about New Orleans's future that were susceptible both to dispute and to accusations of racial bias. How could you be sure population densities were going to be insufficient? And might that not be a self-fulfilling prophecy, calculated to keep blacks from returning to New Orleans? Might that not be Mr. Canizaro's way of assembling large tracts of land on the cheap for massive redevelopment? (p. 316, 2006)

But, I have gotten ahead of my story. Before discussing the 'footprint' controversy related to the ULI recommendations, let's back track a bit to provide full context. As noted in Barbara Kreisler's opening article "A Rude Awakening" in **Urban Land** magazine's January 2006 24-page special report on the Gulf Coast:

> *In the first three months following the hurricane, the city*
> *government mobilized. The mayor appointed the Bring*
> *New Orleans Back (BNOB) Commission, a task force of*
> *influential leaders, all known for their investment in the*
> *city or their political influence, or both. Named as the*
> *chair of the BNOB Commission's committee on city and*
> *urban planning, for example, was real estate developer*
> *Joseph Canizaro, president of New Orleans-based Colum-*
> *bus Properties, whose prominence and connections are*
> *well known in New Orleans. (p. 54, 2006)*

Kreisler goes on to note that the 17-member BNOB Commission was charged with examining the issues most critical to rebuilding the city. These issues included, economic development, culture, government effectiveness, urban planning and development, infrastructure, health care and education. The BNOB had as its charge "To finalize a master plan to advise, assist, and plan the direct funding of the rebuilding of New Orleans culturally, socially, economically, and uniquely for every citizen." In addition to Canizaro and Oliver Thomas, the Commission included members such as New Orleans native Wynton Marsalis, Boysie Bollinger of Bollinger Shipyards, Inc., Tulane University President Scott Cowen, Archbishop Alfred Hughes, Rev. Fred Luter, Jr., community organizer Barbara Major, banker Alden McDonald, among others.

ULI submitted a proposal to BNOB on September 30, 2005 to assist the Commission with its master visioning and planning efforts by creating a strategic framework for an inclusive vision and plan. ULI's proposal stated that this work will be completed through four key activities.

- Forming an Expert Team and an Advisory Panel of national and international experts on post-disaster redevelopment and urban regeneration

- Developing a *Ten Principles for Temporary Communities* publication.

- Engaging the ULI membership at its Fall Meeting in Los Angeles, where over 5,000 members were in attendance.

- Coordinating with other organizations that have dedicated resources to the efforts to rebuild New Orleans.

ULI's proposal further stated that the Expert Team and an Advisory Panel that they assemble will work with the Commission, citizens, stakeholders, and community leaders to develop a strategic framework from which the City can develop its vision and master plan for the future by the end of 2005.

The outline for the strategic framework will be created by the Expert Teams of high level national and international redevelopment professionals and will focus on five of the seven issue areas being addressed by the Commission's subcommittees:

- Economic Development
- Infrastructure
- Administration and Government Efficiency
- City and Urban Planning
- Culture

In addition, ULI will provide advice on how the other two subcommittees (education and health) should be incorporated in the master plan and vision for the city. The Expert Teams and Advisory Panel were in New Orleans from November 12-18, 2005, with the Expert Team working to set the rebuilding framework from November 12 to 14 leaving the Advisory Panel to spend November 14 to 18 touring the city, meeting with the Commission members, city leaders, neighborhood groups, business owners, civic leaders, environmental groups, and other stakeholders to gain their perspectives on the future of the city.

Beginning in October 2005, ULI organized research teams to gather data and information regarding demographics, housing, commercial development, retail and tourism, land use and infrastructure, institutions (universities, hospitals, etc.), environmental resources, and economic development—both pre-Katrina and current. Through these and other methods, the research teams assembled the necessary briefing materials for use by the Expert Team and Advisory Panel. Normally, the sponsor would assemble the briefing book for the Advisory Team, but given the circumstances on the ground in New Orleans, not only did ULI pay for this assignment, but also assembled all the necessary material to make the assignment fruitful. In essence, ULI became both the sponsor and the advisor on this assignment.

At the ULI Fall Meeting in Los Angeles from November 1-4, 2005, for those of us in attendance who were asked to serve on the Expert Team and/or Advisory Panel by ULI's Vice President of Advisory Services, Mary Beth Corrigan, there was an orientation and briefing dinner on November 3, which provided the opportunity to hear an overview of the situation in New Orleans, talk about logistics, and start thinking through the assignment.

At the Fall Meeting, Martha Carr a reporter with the New Orleans Times Picayune was in attendance and spoke with several Expert Team and Advisory Panel members, including myself. Carr's Sunday, November 6, 2005 article "N.O. will need lots of help from federal government," she wrote:

> *"[Tony] Salazer, who co-chaired the rebuilding effort in Los Angeles after the 1993[sic] riots, said there are a handful of companies with a mission to create affordable housing in complex urban areas that are extremely skilled in dealing with local, state and federal government.... You need pioneer people who are willing to come in and take risks to create value..... Urban planner Phil Hart, ..., said the city may want to explore new tactics, like the Parcel-to-parcel concept.....The key is finding ways to leverage the desirable areas of the city to create development in areas that are less attractive. It also gives the black power*

structure a better way of addressing the racial inequities of the past, while building wealth..... The elderly need affordable housing, so do single parents said Jonathon Rose, a developer from Katoneh, N.Y....There are endless amounts of different needs." (p. A-15)

With much anticipation and excitement I took off on a Delta Airlines red eye non-stop flight from Los Angeles International Airport on Friday, November 11th headed for Louis Armstrong International Airport in New Orleans, not knowing what I would see or how I would feel once I arrived. Our first meeting was to be soon after I landed, so I was hoping to sleep a few hours on the flight in order to be fresh. I have been bi-coastal for over a decade, and when I fly from west to east I generally take the red eye flight and work through the following day until I fall fitfully to sleep. It was to be no different for this flight to New Orleans to perhaps the most important assignment in my long career.

As I dozed off to sleep in a window seat in the couch section of the airplane I began dreaming dreams. About one hour out of LAX, the gentleman sitting in front of me seemed to be in distress. His wife, or female companion, was sitting next to him and motioned for a flight attendant to inform her that there was a problem. Immediately, the lights went on throughout the airplane and the flight attendants sprang into action. A call went out to see if there was a physician on board the plane. Fortunately, there was a physician sitting in the first class cabin and he proceed quickly back to the gentlemen seated in front of me. In addition, one of the flight attendants was a registered nurse, so it seemed this gentleman's lucky stars were shining that night. They spent considerable time reviving him and trying to determine the nature of the problem. The crew decided to land in Oklahoma City, Oklahoma in order to take the gentleman off to a waiting ambulance to ferry him to a local hospital. Soon we landed in Oklahoma City, the physician, nurse/flight attendant, and an EMT crew on the ground prepared the man for his exit from the plane. His female companion remained nervously calm as other passengers provided whatever support we could under these circumstances.

I watched closely as the man was placed on a stretcher, taken off the plane, placed in a waiting ambulance headed for an Oklahoma City hospital with his mate. Soon the Delta flight was taxiing down the runway headed for our eventual destination of New Orleans, Louisiana. I did not know if this occurrence was prophetic or not, but it sure did wake me up as I did not sleep for the balance of the flight. To this day I do not know what happened with that gentleman in distress, did he make it or did he not make it? That question still lingers with me, just as that very same question lingers with New Orleans some 18 months after Hurricane Katrina blew threw town waking up an entire city with howling fury and subsequent flooding. Will this distressed city make it or not make it?

Upon landing at Louis Armstrong Airport in New Orleans and de-planing, I ran into a few other ULI folks who were descending on this city in distress like EMTs arriving on the scene to help my unnamed friend on that Delta flight. Current ULI Chair Marilyn Jordan Taylor was arriving from New York City as was Kerrie Rogers, among others. Several of us shared a cab ride to the Sheraton New Orleans on Canal Street, which would be our headquarters over the following week. The hotel was fairly busy when we arrived as displaced staff who worked at the hotel, removal and demolition workers and displaced residents on FEMA housing vouchers, were staying there as well as the many ULI volunteers and staff. If nothing else, the ULI presence was having a significant economic impact on New Orleans as we brought over 100 people to the city for our panel assignment, in addition to the many ULI staffers and senior fellows who had been in New Orleans since October. As we filled up many hotel rooms and ate out at those few French Quarter restaurants that were open, people made it known that they were glad we were there pumping up a crippled economy.

The ULI Expert Team convened at 1PM in the Napoleon C12 Conference Room on the third floor of the hotel for our initial briefing by the ULI staff that had been on the ground for over a month. After the standard introductions of the Expert Team and staff we were presented with a briefing, which supplemented the extensive briefing book we had all received about a week before we arrived in New Orleans. Our briefing materials received before hitting the ground included a summary of stakeholder interviews conducted by the ULI Senior Fellows grouped as an Executive Summary, Economic Development, Culture and Tourism, Local Government Officials, including City Council members, Transportation and Infrastructure, Investors, Bankers, and Insurance Executives, University Officials and Healthcare Providers, Historic Preservation and Environment Groups and Clergy, and Housing and Urban Planning Officials and Grassroots Groups.

In a similar November 8, 2005 e-mail message we received the November 2, online newsletter "The News from Congressman Richard H. Baker, Sixth District, Louisiana," an update where the Congressman answered questions and spells out a vision for his proposed Louisiana Recovery Corporation. Baker saw this proposed legislation as providing a plan to offer economic stability to property owners and facilitate community rebuilding. In this message Cong. Baker (R-Baton Rouge) sought to clarify his bill, a problem that would ultimately plague this legislation until its final death a few months later. A November 8th e-mail also included a message from my good friend and fellow ULI Expert Team and Advisory Panel member Bill Gilchrist in Birmingham, Alabama. Bill in his usual astute and sharing manner recommended that we read Pierce Lewis's *New Orleans: The Making of an Urban Landscape* as a good geographic history of the city. Bill also reminded us that NPR Morning Edition had a piece on the New Orleans town hall meeting that took place in Baton Rouge on November 7th.

I had just seen Bill at the ULI Fall Meeting in Los Angeles, and I looked forward to his multi-lingual, informed contributions to our upcoming, important work in New Orleans. Bill and I had last served together on a ULI Advisory Panel in Camden, New Jersey in June 2004. Also on that panel were ULI Senior Fellow for Housing John McIlwaine who would also be in New Orleans and ULI Trustee and Inner City Advisor for ULI Los Angeles, Michael Banner. Just prior to heading to Camden for that difficult assignment, that city was given the dubious distinction of being 'the most dangerous city in America.' Needless to say, my wife Tanya was thrilled that I was headed to Camden with that moniker awaiting me. Of course, Camden had no suitable hotel to house us so we stayed in Cherry Hill, New Jersey. Incidentally, Michael Banner has been asked by Edward Blakely who was appointed by Mayor Nagin as the Recovery Czar for New Orleans in December 2006 to serve on his advisory committee for recovery starting in June 2006. Also, in the summer of 2005, New Orleans was named 'the most dangerous city in the nation,' thus cementing the ULI reputation of sending the best and the brightest to the worst and most impossible situations.

Clearly, New Orleans was an impossible situation. Plagued by race and class conflict, persistent poverty, a declining economy, rotten public schools, in the midst of water, water everywhere, and glossed over by a veneer of French Quarter good times, the 'Big Easy' was looking at hard times in the aftermath of Mother Nature taking its toll on this vulnerable city. In the midst of this death and despair parachuted 50 post-disaster and redevelopment experts brought in as objective outsiders on ULI's dime to try and lend some balance and sanity to an insane situation.

One definition of insanity is 'senseless.' New Orleans is a senseless tragedy that could have been prevented with better designed, constructed and maintained levees, a better conceived and executed evacuation plan, a more rapid and humane federal response, and most of all human beings better able to communicate with each other and solve problems for the common good.

The Expert Team members then departed the Sheraton New Orleans Hotel at 2:30pm for our first tour of New Orleans. This was one of the most sobering experiences of my life. I had traveled to New Orleans off and on over the years, most frequently to attend the New Orleans Jazz and Heritage Festival in late April and early May of each year, so I was somewhat familiar with the city and its neighborhoods. What I saw in the majority of these neighborhoods where flooding was most severe was shocking. There were some neighborhoods, such as in the Lower 9th Ward, where we could not even get off the bus! Trees, debris, trash, cars, trucks, refrigerators, were everywhere. On two story houses you could see the brackish, brown color of the water line. On one-story houses you did not see the stain as the water was over the roof.

As we drove through New Orleans East I saw a neighborhood much like the one I grew up in Denver, Colorado. Brick homes with yards, but largely abandoned with front doors either swinging open or gone entirely. Front windows were broken and many homes looked as if they had been looted and ransacked. As we drove through this neighborhood I could envision people outside watering their lawns, children riding bikes on the sidewalks and streets, a bustle of activity that was now only a vacant memory. Where were these people? Why did this happen to these people? A predominantly African American middle class community laid low by Katrina and breaches in the levees, or perhaps as Jed Horne puts it a 'Breach of Faith'—faith that hard work will pay off in the end, faith that your duly elected officials are looking out for your interests.

I felt similar feelings when we rode through the predominantly middle class white community of Lakeview. This neighborhood was similarly laid low by the water rushing through the levees from Lake Pontchartrain to the north. Separated by City Park, Lakeview and New Orleans East seemed separated by more than green space, but by a vast racial divide that sometimes gets in the way of sensible, sane decision-making. Two similar neighborhoods, two dissimilar worlds, both floating underwater while their inhabitants fled to distant places.

Volunteer
By Ed Rosenthal

The teacher at that school
With the empty yard
A black woman
In a white blouse
and a black skirt
With curly snake hair
stared through glasses
above her beak

She leaned on her arm
bent at the elbow
on a short metal fence
And looked at the dirt
Where no kids ran
or screamed at all.

She thought of her Dad
Shoulders hunched over
in his work clothes
kicking a shovel
with his heel
into sandy soil back home.
Green weeds
with yellow faces
hunched over
and smirked behind his back.

That night she dreamt an orange cloudburst
flashed inside a black squall
Fruits vegetables
and children in jumpers
fell from the sky
and filled angular boats
on the levees.
The sky was a yellow sun
The air was electric

She opened her eyes
And raised her hands to heaven
She raised her cell
off her plain stand
to called a freckle faced redhead
she'd met cleaning
the counters of a makeshift market
Who had whispered to her
with passion
about a voluntary soup kitchen

"I'm in.", she told her.

Touring Lakeview and New Orleans East hardly prepared us for what we saw when we arrived in the Lower 9th Ward. Here we saw houses picked up by the foundation and thrown asunder, cars and trucks crushed under houses, trash and debris everywhere, along with a foul odor that spoke of mold, toxic water and death. We could not even depart the bus in the Lower 9th; we could only view the devastation from the safety of the tour bus. I thought again of those without the means who had to make it on foot from the Lower

9th to either the Louisiana Superdome or the Morial Convention Center in the midst of hurricane winds and flooding—what a miracle of faith and perseverance and a will to live. For it is by no means a short walk from the Lower 9th to the Central Business District where both 'houses of refuge' lay.

When we at last arrived back at the hotel after this grueling tour, I felt exhausted! I retreated to my room and called my wife back in Los Angeles to try and describe what I had just seen. It was virtually impossible to describe the devastation in one telephone conversation. We then came together again at 6pm and headed out walking to dinner at Muriel's Jackson Square. This was a working dinner and was quite productive after we discussed the shock of what we had just seen throughout this crippled city. After dinner we made our way back to the hotel from the French Quarter on foot, a few of us encountered Ray Nagin coming out of a restaurant along the way. We stopped and introduced ourselves as members of the ULI panel in town to try and assist the city. Nagin seemed pleased to see us and we chatted with him for a while before we departed in different directions. Little did I know that this would be an omen of later events as we would again depart in different directions in relationship to strategies to rebuild New Orleans.

On Sunday, November 13, the Expert Team continued its work starting with a working session at 9am, which then led to a working lunch at noon culminating with an additional working session at 1pm. At 4:30pm the Advisory Panel members who had recently come into town joined the Expert Team for an organizational meeting. We then adjourned for dinner at 6:30pm at Loews New Orleans on Poydras Street in the LaFourche/Pointe Coupee room on the 9th floor. Mayor Ray Nagin joined us for dinner and made some remarks. Perhaps the strongest words that night were delivered by Pittsburgh, Pennsylvania Mayor Thomas Murphy, who was a member of the Expert Team and Advisory Panel. Mayor Murphy talked about making difficult decisions and doing what you think is right. He was clearly directing his comments toward Mayor Nagin, who left before dinner was finished.

As we walked back to the Sheraton New Orleans Hotel we were talking about what we had heard and what we were seeing on the streets in front of us. As a group of us walking together approached the entrance to the hotel, we noticed that there were a couple of police cars in front. A small crowd had gathered to see what was going on in a city where everything was seemingly going wrong. As we got closer, the police were bringing an African American male, perhaps 40-45 years old, out of the hotel in handcuffs. He was sweating and apologizing profusely. It seems he had run into the hotel threatening to commit suicide, changed his mind, and then the police came on the scene and pulled him out of the hotel and put him in one of the squad cars. We could only imagine what had driven this man to such an extreme measure. We all knew the gravity of the situation in the city, and this incident merely drove the point home all the more. Distress was everywhere. It was in the air, the people, the streets, and the buildings. Could we be of any help to a city in such distress?

By Monday, November 14th, a few members of the Expert Team that were not on the Advisory Panel had headed back home. Being a part of both teams, I was still there trying to best determine how to help a very sick patient. The remaining members of the Expert Team then reported out to the Advisory Panel at 8am in our usual spot, Napoleon C12 on the Third Floor of the hotel. All I could think of was "Napoleon and Waterloo." However, I was able to focus once we began reporting out on our "Bring New Orleans Back Strategy."

For each area we focused on main themes, core issues, recommended strategies and a plan for long-term success. So for example, in what would prove to be the most controversial portion of our work dealing with city and urban planning, that team had as main themes, build upon the best for which New Orleans is known; balance engineered systems and natural systems to achieve safety;

plan system implementation that allows rebuilding to begin as soon as possible; plan holistically, act incrementally, measure efficaciously. As to core issues, the city and urban planning team suggested, establish criteria for neighborhood reconstruction and land use to identify what should be maintained, restored, be something new; require fine grain intervention where damage was episodic; require broader changes in land-use due to more pervasive damage; determine the initial post-Katrina footprint that creates a better city; appreciate how the range and blend of environmental and engineering approaches toward flood protection informs short-range, mid-range, and long-range land use changes that are sustainable, economical and reflective of the communities values and culture; account for the racial and ethnic diversity of New Orleans in a credible manner that speaks process and outcome, including but not limited to the right to return—although perhaps to a different, safer location; plan for the right public and private sector partnerships to make it happen; ensure that critical public services fulfill their potential in the plan's success.

Recommended strategies during this early phase of our work as captured in the Expert Team report for city and urban planning included, the importance of neighborhood participation, i.e., neighborhood planning units, churches as key players; make the case, i.e., demonstrate robust local effort to assist New Orleans's case for federal assistance; speed in terms of restoral of basic services, insurance payouts and housing; get stranded institutions back on line; and plan now for a new model in primary education.

As to a plan for long-term success, the Expert Team discussed the best structure to plan the work and work the plan; build on the 'specialized difference' of New Orleans; and build the economic, social and cultural rebirth of the city on its unique past.

Each of the other Expert Teams followed this same reporting format in its session with the Advisory Panel members. This presentation in concert with the voluminous briefing book and key stakeholder interviews along with a tour of the city allowed the Expert Team to set the table for the Advisory Panel's work in the next phase of this assignment.

The Advisory Panel members then took a bus tour of the devastated city after a briefing and then lunch. I decided to take the tour for a second time to ensure I had not been hallucinating the day before. It was again a very sobering experience that reinforced in my mind both the force of Mother Nature and the frailty of the human race.

Once the tour was completed, a sober, quiet group of dedicated professionals arrived back at the hotel for a 5pm working dinner in anticipation of the Town Hall Meeting scheduled for 6pm at the Sheraton New Orleans in the Napoleon B123 ballroom. Over 300 people showed up for this meeting, in addition to press from around the world. The over 50 Advisory Panel members sat behind a long raised dais and listened for hours as people with a variety of tales of horror and hope paraded to the microphones spread strategically throughout the room.

We heard from over seventy people from almost every neighborhood in the city. They had stories of woe and loss and recommendations to improve a new New Orleans. We heard from City Council President Oliver Thomas who reiterated that New Orleans was one of the top destinations in the world, we heard from City Councilwoman Cynthia Ward-Lewis who represents New Orleans East and the Lower 9th Ward who advocated the right to return, and we even had a hex placed on us group of 'outsiders' by a woman I can only identify as speaker number thirty nine even as she bespoke of conspiracy theories, racism and echoing Oliver Thomas that New Orleans was a key destination. Ironically, speaker number thirty-nine was the only person among over seventy speakers who addressed the panel who neither offered her name or which neighborhood she lived in. I have a list, which I made that tense night of the name of each person who addressed the panel and their neighborhood of residence in my Sheraton New Orleans note pad.

Weary and tired after the town meeting, which adjourned at around 11:30pm, I hustled to my room to call my wife just to get a sense of how normal things were in the Hollywood neighborhood we called home. I then turned in for the night dreaming of being the victim of a hex here in the midst of Cajun country.

The next day, Tuesday, November 15th, we had team interviews scheduled from 8am to 5pm, with lunch and an interview debriefing being our only respite. I was assigned to the Economic Development and Culture team. Among my team members was Kerrie Rogers; and those individuals she and I interviewed were drawn from the economic development and culture worlds in New Orleans. We interviewed a significant number of people in the four-hour time period. We heard from a white investment banker who said that Katrina accelerated an inevitable decline and that the city budget needed to be right-sized as pre-Katrina the city budget of $600 million was pegged to a city of one million, not one of 465,000. He also commented that the business community was concerned about the lack of political leadership and the race issue.

We interviewed an African American public relations and advertising executive who is a lifelong resident of the city and remembers Hurricane Betsy in 1963. He stated that it would be a longer recovery period than most people expect, and that the economy has to diversify. We heard from the director of tourism who noted that people love New Orleans for its authenticity and that convention business saw a big decline since 2002. She also reminded us that in the summer of 2005 New Orleans became the murder capital of the nation, always a bad sign for the tourism industry. An attorney and real estate developer who serves on the BNOB told us that the city needed to bring back the black people who work in the culture and tourism industry. A noted restaurateur reminded us that the city's culinary image does not just come from downtown and that many neighborhood restaurants were flooded out and may not re-open. The head of design and construction for Harrah's noted that the city's brain drain was occurring before Katrina. All these interviews with these diverse people revealed a love for New Orleans, but concern over what the city had become even before Katrina blew into town.

On Wednesday, November 16th we began an all day working session to begin putting our presentation together scheduled in two days. We worked in our teams from 8am through dinner on report production. This same grueling, intense, intellectual and heated work continued on Thursday, November 17th beginning at 8am and continuing well into the night. We all knew we were putting together an important report that would receive local, national and international press scrutiny on Friday morning. More importantly, we all knew we wanted to present objective recommendations that could move this distressed city forward in a positive manner. We also knew that the most important part of our presentation the next morning would be those recommendations dealing with a repopulation strategy for the city. Joe Brown, CEO of EDAW in San Francisco, led our efforts for the city and urban planning team.

We tinkered that evening with the order of the presentation. Advisory Panel chair Smedes York had been doing a masterful job in managing this large, talented and concerned group on land use professionals as we dealt with our own emotions in the midst of this challenging assignment. Patrick Phillips who chaired the economic development and culture team asked me to make our public presentation the following morning. I was pleased and flattered to be given this assignment and began focusing on this task.

Initially we had discussed opening with the economic development and culture section of the power point presentation after Smedes made his opening remarks. After much discussion, we decided to have government effectiveness follow Smedes, with economic development and culture following as the second presentation.

Each team ran through their presentations, which had been written, revised, re-written, revised, over and over the last two days. We then turned our attention to Joe Brown and his presentation, which like the others, had been re-worked over and over again the last two days. There was much debate and discussion as to how best present both the oral and visual aspects of our city and urban planning recommendations. With the group of post-disaster and redevelopment experts in the room ranging from post-earthquake and riots in Los Angeles to post-9/11 in New York City to reviving the Steel City of Pittsburgh to post-neighborhood razing in Boston represented, we finally concluded after several viewings of Joe's slides and critiquing his accompanying remarks that we had no choice but to call it as we saw it. That is, the level of damage varied across the city and across neighborhoods. It would not be possible to rebuild the more heavily damaged areas of the city at the same pace as the less damaged areas of the city. Of course, the more extensive damage tended to be found in those areas of the city that were below sea level. These also tended to be the areas of the city that were largely populated by African Americans.

At one point in our discussion about how to best present this set of recommendations, someone in the group, perhaps Joe Brown, remarked about how we should present this set of recommendations in less than twelve hours from now in such a way that we do not get run out of town. I then remarked, "Sometimes it's okay to get run out of town." This comment served as a reality check on the important task standing before us. It was not taken nor intended as a humorous comment, but reflected one of the big challenges usually facing ULI panels when we make recommendations for redevelopment, some of which may not be received kindly. Given the dire circumstances facing New Orleans, this particular recommendation would be the centerpiece of our redevelopment strategies. We then turned to fine-tuning our public presentation knowing that this one aspect of our work could damage the entire public report.

But I felt Joe Brown would be the ideal person to tell this part of the story on our behalf.

During this lengthy day I also continued to remind the Advisory Panel that we had to take into account the racial dimension in both our presentation on Friday and our subsequent report. I noted my work on cities, suburbs and blacks with James Blackwell, not knowing at that point that he had too become a Katrina evacuee. I reinforced the sense of distrust and alienation attendant to the African American experience in not only New Orleans, but also the United States as a whole. The other African American panel members helped make the case for taking into account the message we delivered to address the concerns of this racial group who were 2 out of every 3 persons in New Orleans pre-Katrina. In addition to Bill Gilchrist from Birmingham, there was Oscar Harris a noted urban planner and architect from Atlanta, and Virginia Fields Manhattan Borough President, who stood with me on this issue.

Later in the evening as we started our presentation rehearsal at 6pm, I suggested that we needed to add a bit of evangelical zeal to our remarks. I attend a Pentecostal church, West Angeles Church of God in Christ in Los Angeles, so each Sunday I am exposed to the dynamic preaching of Bishop Charles E. Blake, which I was using as an example for our presentation. There were other great black preachers who spoke at West Angeles, such as Bishop T.D. Jakes from Dallas, Bishop Charles Brown and Bishop Paul Morton, both from New Orleans. In fact, the Sunday before I departed for New Orleans, Bishop Brown was the guest preacher. He spoke of losing both his church and his house in the flood. Granted, architects, developers, public officials, mayors, and the others charged with making our presentation are not black preachers, but I was merely trying to encourage us to think about how we present our message, ala Bishop Blake, Jakes, Morton and most importantly in this instance, Bishop Charles Brown.

In addition, I pointed out that it is like we are preaching to a predominantly black congregation. Given the historic place of this racial group in this society, distress, pain, and despair are routinely found in their church pews, thus motivating the black preacher to deliver a message of healing to enable them to make it through the week. Further, given that I attend many programs every year where real estate developers, architects and engineers, elected officials, et al, make presentations that are routinely dull, I wanted to inject some thought as to dynamism in our presentations. For, surely, the next morning we were going to be addressing an audience in need of healing.

Knowing we each had 12-15 minutes for our presentation, which included remarks accompanying a PowerPoint slide, I then charted a course for delivering my message related to economic development and culture. I started with The Message discussing our theme of Restoration, Reform and Rebirth. I then went into the Word, which embodies The Problem and Alternatives, then moved into my Summary, which includes Hard Decisions and The Need for Focused Leadership and a Focused Process. Then came the Altar Call and Pass the Plate where I described tough choices, a smaller city and economic development directions.

Of course my content was economic development and culture. But my goal was to tell a story in an evangelical manner. I mulled over how I would begin my remarks—and began thinking of the storm analogy—always good with a message of healing. I also knew that I would be leading into introducing Bill Gilchrist and the city and urban planning team report, so I became conscious of an appropriate segue into this most crucial part of our recommendations.

As our presentation rehearsal drew further into the night, I continued to press my case that we needed to tailor our message for a city that was racially divided and skeptical of 'white voices.' In addition, taking off from New Orleans as a destination, a theme we had heard many times over the past few days, I compared this city with another known destination—my neighborhood of Hollywood, California. I also emphasized that like Hollywood, New Orleans is a brand known worldwide. How can the city leverage this brand in its redevelopment process, just as Hollywood has done over the past decade, partially with the help of ULI. I also re-emphasized the need to present our respective content in a dynamic, informative and inclusive manner—much like the black preacher on Sunday morning.

Although we went through several drafts of our presentation over the course of the day, our draft produced at 9:15am provides a good snapshot of our thinking regarding the most controversial issue of city and urban planning.

This Thursday morning draft stated that, "The planning process is critical in determining New Orleans's best approach to sanction future land-use patterns as part of a recovery process and for the city's long-term public interest. This report will posit a range of technical evaluations that constitute criteria for future land-use. From this evaluation strategy, other approaches for neighborhood reinvestment, rehabilitation, and repopulation will be proposed. The determination process proposed in this report is derived through practical and measurable criteria. Moreover, this process must be applied equally across all areas within the city to ensure fair treatment for all citizens.

Criteria for the assessment of property for future land-use policy would include:

- Flood extents and depths
- Topography
- Canals/levees pumping system capacity
- Owner occupancy
- Current building condition
- Number of previous flood incidents
- Storm sewer system capacity
- Historic district designation
- Repeated incidents of damage

Other valid criteria may emerge to inform the best use of land towards an overall strategy of a safe and viable city. At the core of this methodology lies a basic understanding that flood impacts vary across and within neighborhoods and that even in the unprecedented case of Katrina, all flooding was not equally destructive. Therefore, any assessment will encounter instances where damage occurred sporadically within some neighborhoods, while being extensive over entire areas in others. Post-Katrina property damage will also range from mildly impacted to severely damaged and destroyed.

As a result of these assessments and their possible outcomes, we should expect the need for replacement housing and reprogramming of land for other public purposes, primarily open space.

Each of these approaches (to land use) will support a planning theme to respect the New Orleans's character block-by-block to develop sustainable systems of infrastructure including storm water management, and to engage neighborhoods as the basic planning unit."

In saying this, we knew that anything but 'restore the city block-by-block exactly as it was right before Katrina', would receive mixed reviews. It was as if people wanted God to snap his fingers and put Humpty Dumpty back together again exactly as before—but that was not possible. Unless of course, speaker number thirty nine possessed the power to not only place a hex on the ULI outsiders bent on helping rebuild her city, but also to restore her city in its exact pre-Katrina configuration with a blink of her eye.

We broke up around midnight. I headed to my room to prepare my remarks in front of a mirror. A group of others who were not presenters the next morning headed out to try and catch Irving Mayfield at a local joint before curfew set in. Yes, the Big Easy was coming back in the above sea level neighborhoods such as the French Quarter.

I slept for about five hours that night, going over in my dreams how the presentation would go in a few hours. The next morning, breakfast was available at 7am in the Maurepas Room. Our report presentation was scheduled for 9am in the Napoleon Ballroom— and would be open to the public and press.

When I arrived at the Napoleon Ballroom at 8:45am, the room was filling up. Press from around the world was either already in place or in the process of setting up. We started a bit after 9am as our chairman Smedes York called the meeting to order. I was sitting near Smedes as I was one of the prescribed presenters. I looked down from the dais noting several BNOB Commissioners sitting on the front row…I counted ten in all. There were also a couple of City Councilors, including Cynthia Ward-Lewis who had seen nearly a dozen family members lose their homes in this disaster. I did not see Mayor Ray Nagin. He was evidently in Washington, D.C. meeting with federal officials.

As an aside, before reporting on what was said and its aftermath, I must comment on Mayor Nagin. As I noted earlier, he was one part of a perfect storm that has exacerbated the New Orleans Katrina disaster. A cable television executive and native of New Orleans, when Nagin took office in 2002 this was his first elective office. Thus, in Katrina's aftermath New Orleans was saddled with a well meaning Mayor intent on rooting out the traditional cronyism and patronage in the pre-Katrina New Orleans, now sitting atop a city bureaucracy that was crumbling and near bankruptcy.

The neighborhood I grew up in within Denver produced two mayors of big cities in recent history. Both African American and products of Manual High School in Northeast Denver, Wellington Webb served three terms in Denver and Norman Rice served two terms in Seattle. Both these cities did not have anything close to African American majorities when Webb and Rice took the reins. I observed both my childhood friends govern with authority and decisiveness, though granted neither had experienced anything like

Hurricane Katrina. But I surmise, if they had, both Webb and Rice would have been better prepared for such a challenge than is Nagin.

While living in Boston I taught at the University of Massachusetts, Boston for over 25 years. One of my students, Tom Menino, was raised in the Hyde Park section of the city, dropped out of college before graduating, began working in the public sector, came back to college, got elected to the Boston City Council where he became President, then took over as Mayor when Ray Flynn was appointed as U.S. Ambassador to the Vatican in 1993.

Some fourteen years later, Tom Menino is still the Mayor of Boston and dubbed by some as 'Mayor for Life.' He was my student in UMass-Boston's College of Public and Community Service (CPCS), a program for older undergraduates who have a wealth of lifetime experience and needed or wanted a college degree. Tom and I used to sit in my office and his office in Boston City Hall talking politics, neighborhoods, and cities. When Tom first ran for Mayor in 1993, I recall returning from a morning class to my office where I fielded a telephone call from a reporter from the Boston Globe inquiring about Tom Menino, the college student. His rival James Brett had an Ivy League education, while Tom merely graduated from a public university in 1988 after dropping out of college at an earlier age. I dutifully vouched for Tom; he defeated Brett and has yet to look back.

The reason I relate my experiences in Denver and in Boston, is that I know big city mayors and what it takes to be an effective municipal leader. Sad to say, I have not yet seen these leadership qualities in Ray Nagin. I do hope they have been lying dormant and that they will soon reveal themselves, for whatever one thinks of the ULI recommendations, New Orleans is crying out for leadership that can make a difference.

Now back to the Napoleon Ballroom at the Sheraton New Orleans Hotel on Friday, November 18, 2005. Cribbing from Guillermo's

Notes from this ULI presentation, I provide the following summary of his comments.

- Carl Weisbrod—President, Real Estate Division, Trinity Church, New York City.

- Tom Murphy—Mayor of Pittsburgh, PA.

- Virginia Fields—President, Borough of Manhattan.

- Philip Hart—President/CEO, Hart Realty Advisors, Hollywood, CA.

- William Gilchrist—Director, Dept. of Planning, Engineering & Permits, City of Birmingham, AL.

- Joseph Brown, EDAW, Inc., San Francisco, CA.

- Warren Whitlock—Director, Construction Coordination, Columbia University, New York City.

- Tony Salazer—President, West Coast Division, McCormack Baron Salazar, Los Angeles, CA.

Weisbrod, Murphy and Fields were presenting on Government Effectiveness. I was presenting on Economic Development and Culture. Gilchrist and Brown were presenting on city and urban planning. Whitlock was presenting on infrastructure. Salazar was presenting on housing. Of this lineup, there were four African Americans (Fields, Hart, Gilchrist and Whitlock) and one Latino (Salazar), along with three white males. I point this fact out as we are not yet a colorblind society despite the protestations of Ward Connerly and Shelby Steele, and the like.

Carl Weisbrod had served on the ULI Hollywood, California panel in March 2001 that I co-sponsored. Bill Gilchrist and I served together on a ULI panel in Camden, New Jersey in June 2004 as noted earlier. I had full confidence in Carl, Bill, and the other presenters on this important day in the history of both ULI and the City of New Orleans.

Carl Weisbrod

- Funding from federal agencies is necessary and ULI will help to get that funding.

- Implementation should happen through a new body, the Crescent City Rebuilding Corporation.

- Federal assistance should be geared towards helping small businesses, rebuilding infrastructure, port facilities, environmental remediation, and for grants, loans, and tax cuts for historical buildings.

- Inspiration to design these recovery systems should be drawn from the lessons from New York after 9/11.

- The existing redevelopment authority is too weak at this moment to be the leader in the reconstruction and recovery.

- To lead this corporation a high quality CEO with political and managerial skills should be hired.

- The Crescent Corporation should inspire the citizens and the government.

- Utility recovery is critical. ENTERGY must be supported and there should be a special appropriation of funds to repair and expand the electricity rate base.

- Funds should be given for planning in neighborhoods to strengthen and empower the different parts of the city, besides the larger city effort.

Tom Murphy

- The rules (policies) need to be changed in order to succeed in the reconstruction; therefore, they propose a new financial oversight board.

- "The tax structure stink" (lit) in New Orleans just the same as in Pittsburgh.

- Change is possible as is it was in Pittsburgh, where the city was changed from a steel industry city to a place where only 5% of the workforce works in heavy industry.

- It won't be easy because there are interests that want to keep the rules as they are.

- Seven members of the board for governance should be elected by the President, Governor, Mayor, and City Council.

- Use existing techniques like COMSTAT to measure the level of efficiency in city services delivery.

Virginia Fields

- Greater transparency and communication are needed.

Philip Hart

- Focus on the cultural aspects to promote economic development.

- Facilitate capacity building.

- There was little growth in the city of New Orleans before the storm. Try to change that in this opportunity by helping people get back on their feet and establish the foundation for growth.

- One needs to consider these: Workforce, leadership, equity, culture, capital, and have a strategy.

- Small businesses are the backbone of the economy. Enable short-term access to capital, outreach, and centralize information and resource bases.

- In the long-term: ensure public and private investment, foster entrepreneurship, and a strategic plan. Increase capacity and establish priorities.

- Small businesses need to participate actively in the rebuilding process.

- There needs to be workforce development so that the city creates skilled workers.

- There needs to be outreach to displaced residents.

- Bring back musicians, find venues for them to perform, and expand the pool of cultural ambassadors for the city.

- Many musicians have lost their equipment, so establish a fund to help them recover their equipment.

- Bioscience is a forte in the city: Secure funding for key initiatives.

- Lure faculty and students to strengthen the highly skilled specialized workforce.

William Gilchrist

- Plan for the challenges ahead.

- Recovery will occur under the flood protection assumption. This protection needs to be at a level that ensures the safety of the people.

- The neighborhoods' integrity needs to be kept. That means rebuilding and reoccupying completely. If not, people will not return.

- Ensure safe and secure neighborhoods.

Joseph Brown

- Planning and rebuilding works if all the other plans are good as examples in England and elsewhere have shown.

- Wetlands of New Orleans region have been lost to a great extent in this event.

- To the East, the water is at the gates of the city because the wetland is gone after Katrina.

- Partially submerged vegetation and soil builds a protective barrier and now it is mostly gone because of Katrina.

- The city is largely home-owned showing the multi-generational rooting to the city.

- Strategy for action: Sequential investment areas, waters, levees, canals, strategic open spaces that allow for flooding and quick cleaning afterwards.

- Topography: New Orleans must rediscover the natural ridges that exist in the city. They can help define future levees.

- Depth of inundation: Not all the neighborhoods that flooded did so equally. Some suffered small flooding, some flooded enormously.

- Connecting corridors. It's not enough to have a perimeter protection, you need an interior protections systems and open spaces to have a new relationship to water. These interior spaces can serve as inundation planes (especially those topographically low) that connect to wetlands in the east, without damaging the city.

- Reinvestment strategy is suggested to occur in three phases. Get back quickly and re-stabilize homes. Some parts look OK superficially but they have systems that are in bad shape.

- Sequential reinvestment approach with priorities to certain zones.

- Work with communities and churches, etc.

Warren Whitlock

- Recovery stage should occur from now until 1-year anniversary of Katrina.

- Rebuilding stage in years 1-5.

- Growing stage between 2010-2018, the year of New Orleans' tri-centennial anniversary.

- Use the Louisiana Recovery Authority Smart Growth Principles.

- Be careful with environmental risk equity. Do not dump toxic materials or rubble in poor neighborhoods; share the risks.

- Infrastructural: Improve flood protection, transit networks, environmental systems, and utilities.

Tony Salazar

- Conduct a survey of buildings to understand what is there so that we can define the challenge for future construction and repairs.

- Activate the Crescent City Rebuilding Corporation.

- Need immediate temporary housing with adequate open spaces and utilities.

- Getting people in is a priority.

- Get all available housing units into the market. A housing authority needs to reoccupy the buildings that are in higher ground and prepare them for use.

- Design guidelines for owners to renovate and repair appropriately.

- Pre-qualify contractors so that homeowners will not get ripped off.

- Understand that housing is now a public resource, a limited commodity.

- Establish training facilities for people to become skilled in the reconstruction.

- Re-evaluate building codes. Make it uniform and make it known.

- Establish an OMBUDS office so that people know there is a place for answers.

- Fight for the postponing of mortgage payments for property owners. Crescent City Rebuilding Corp. should treat everybody equally and fairly.

- The corporation will serve as a "land bank."

- Fair compensation must be given for all homeowners, returning or not.

Guillermo's Notes captured the essence of our presentation. Besides the notes for Joe Brown's presentation, Guillermo stated: "This presentation was great!" However, not everyone was as enamored with Joe's excellent presentation. As is custom with such gatherings, elected officials are given the first opportunity to speak. Smedes called on City Councilwoman Cynthia Ward-Lewis who rose to speak in her black Baptist preacher voice and cadence. But almost with her first words I knew that she either misunderstood or did not comprehend the depth and scope of Joe's presentation and recommendations. This was the first sign of trouble for our recommendations, for Councilwoman Lewis did not understand our repopulation strategy and reinvestment sequence. . In addition, it was as if no other presentations had been made other than Joe's. Fortunately, many others in the vast crowd, including BNOB member, Barbara Majors, seemed to fully understand the scope of what we presented and commended us on the depth and care for the city expressed in our work.

We then adjourned the presentation as the press scampered to get reactions from the ULI volunteers as well as others gathered that morning. ULI Chair Marilyn Jordan Taylor escorted a few of us upstairs to a press conference with local, national and international press. As we entered the room Marilyn embraced Joe, acknowledging his excellent presentation under such difficult circumstances. We then sat down to face the press. I sat right next to Joe and patted him on the back. Smedes took to the podium and introduced us and the press conference began. As anticipated, the bulk of the press questions were directed to Joe. Obviously, the question of a strategy to repopulate the city's neighborhoods was a key concern and would overshadow all other elements of our recommendations. However, the key point Smedes kept reinforcing was that our work was not the end, but the beginning—which was an appropriate and accurate thing to say. For the value of ULI's 60-year old Advisory Services Program is its objectivity, accuracy and responsiveness to over 400 communities worldwide. New Orleans was perhaps the most difficult of any of the previous assignments, but we had done our job and had done it well. It was now up to the locals working in concert with state and federal officials to forge a master plan that could gain consensus and lead the rebuilding efforts in New Orleans. This would be the ultimate test for a devastated city where the art of gaining political consensus was difficult even in the best of times.

On the Friday, November 18, 2005, of the ULI recommendations for strategies for rebuilding New Orleans, *New Orleans Times Picayune* staff writer Martha Carr's byline was, "Consultants to City: Shrink livable areas."

Carr writes:

> *"In the most comprehensive recovery plan proposed to date, a panel of more than 50 specialists in urban and post-disaster planning said New Orleans should concentrate its rebuilding efforts on the sections of the city that occupy the high ground, while securing lower-lying areas for potential rebirth in the long-term.*

Tackling what is certain to be the most controversial aspect of any rebuilding plan, the contingent from the Urban Land Institute said Friday that the city should use its original footprint, as well as lessons learned from Hurricane Katrina, as a guide in determining what areas are most logical for redevelopment. Firing off a collection of bold ideas, the group also proposed creating a public development corporation that would buy and sell property to speed the city's redevelopment; establishing an oversight board with broad powers over the city's finances; and engineering a secondary flood-control network inside the city that would use natural ridges, levees, water reservoirs, and green space to stop widespread flooding.

The panelists, many of whom helped rebuild cities like New York after 9/11 and Los Angeles after the Northridge earthquake in 1994, said it's not practical to redevelop every acre of New Orleans in the sort term, considering that 300,000 residents and 160,000 jobs have been lost. It's also not socially equitable to allow residents back into neighborhoods that do not have adequate levee protection and may be toxic.

The group went so far as to draft a color-coded map of the city showing three 'investment zones' the city may want to follow. The first zone included the high parts of the city, like Uptown and the French Quarter, which panelists say is ready for rehabilitation immediately. The second zone highlighted the Mid-ground, which the panel suggested is also ready for individual rehabilitation, with some opportunities to put together parcels of land for green space or redevelopment.

Maps and Graphics

historic growth

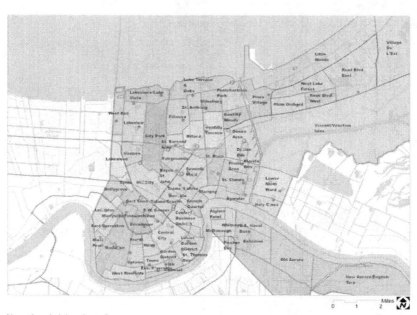

city of neighborhoods

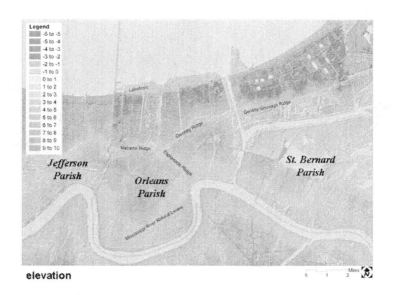

elevation

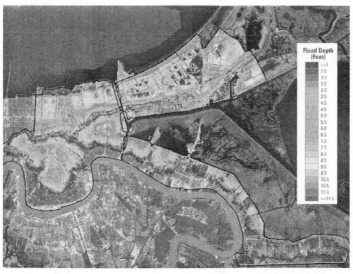

flood inundation

source: USGS

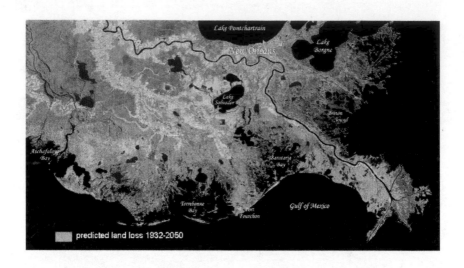

water at the city gates

The last zone, which included some of the cities hardest hit neighborhoods, needs additional study, but could have the potential for mass buyouts and future green space, the panel said. Those areas include most of New Orleans east, Gentilly and Desire; the northern part of Lakeview; and parts of the Lower 9th Ward, Broadmoor, Mid-City and Hollygrove. In those neighborhoods, the panel emphasized that all homeowners should be compensated for their property at pre-Katrina values. They also stressed that if the worst-hit areas are allowed to redevelop in a scattershot way, homeowners will begin to rehab houses on partially abandoned streets, creating the shanty towns with little to no property value.

The panel's map also included green areas running along natural ridges and between neighborhoods, where members suggest creating a network of flood-protection measures, from inner-city levees to new parks, to reduce the risk of flooding and stop waters from blanketing the city.

While the proposal was immediately questioned by New Orleans City Councilwoman, Cynthia Willard-Lewis, who represents Eastern New Orleans and the Lower 9th Ward, others attending the panel's presentation were more receptive to the idea, but questioned whether the political will exists to make it happen,.

When the panel concluded its hour-long presentation, members of Nagin's commission said they were extremely impressed by the detail of the draft report and the panel's wealth of ideas. While the ULI panel stopped short of advocating a merger of Nagin's commission and Gov. Blanco's Louisiana Recovery Authority, it did stress that city and state leaders must craft a single vision, and move more quickly in their rebuilding efforts.

'I appreciate your bluntness,' said commission co-chair Barbara Major. 'You have challenged us to make more difficult and controversial choices..... There has to be some behavioral changes across the board. I think we just have to kick a little butt and do what we have to do."

Thus far, the elected officials in the city of New Orleans have not been willing to kick a little butt and make some behavioral changes in the midst of this particular crisis. Real leadership that has the whole city in mind that is not driven by strictly political consider-ations has been lacking. In addition, the primary sticking point has been moving forward on a realistic strategy for repopulating the city neighborhood-by-neighborhood. The ULI strategy for repop-ulation emphasized the need for both individual and collective action depending upon the level of devastation. Thus far, the indi-vidual action has far outpaced the collective action.

Further, the reaction to the ULI repopulation strategy has diverted attention away from the substance of other recommendations the panel made. As noted in the January 2006 issue of **Urban Land** magazine, the essential elements to spur rebuilding and to ensure the city's long-term viability includes:

- Recognition that every citizen has a right to return to a safe city, with enhanced levees and ecosystem restoration playing a key role in ensuring future safety.

- Recognition of the need for diverse economic development that results in creation of a broader range of jobs that pro-vide a broader salary range; the panel also endorsed a requirement for a livable wage.

- Establishment of a rebuilding corporation—the Crescent City Rebuilding Corporation—to expedite reconstruction of both residential and commercial properties.

- Establishment of a temporary financial oversight board—with members representing the federal, state, and local governments—to ensure fairness and equity in obtaining federal funding.

- Adoption of clear criteria for neighborhood restoration and development, with an emphasis on the inclusion of residents in the planning and restoration.

- Acceptance that diversity, equity and cooperation are keys to rebuilding.

- Recognition of the influence of the faith-based community in maintaining the recovery's momentum.

- Recognition of the need for tax reform and incentives to build up the city's tax base and encourage private investment; and

- Recognition of the need for a regional approach on such critical issues as levees, transportation systems, emergency response, and economic development.

The January 2006 **Urban Land** magazine special report on New Orleans also notes the initial community reaction to ULI's Panel Recommendations:

> *"The release of the panel's report sparked immediate reaction. While planning and redevelopment professionals understood the reasoning behind the panel's recommendation that the city defer redevelopment of properties in severely damaged neighborhoods and focus rebuilding in the safer, higher-ground areas, many of the residents most directly affected opposed any plans that did not include immediate rebuilding in their neighborhoods. Shortly afterward, the City Council voted unanimously to reject the plan and said residents should be allowed to rebuild wherever and whenever they chose. Nonetheless, the*

panel's report stimulated necessary discussions on future rebuilding and served as a springboard for the Bring New Orleans Back Commission's recommendations, which were formally released January 11."

In the December 11, 2005 edition of the Sunday New York Times, a harsh editorial appeared which lamented about the death of an American city. Seemingly, this dire editorial may have been inspired by the behavior of key elected officials and stakeholders in New Orleans in response to the challenges of coming up with a plan to guide the rebuilding process. In that same edition of the *New York Times*, a front page article in the "The Week in Review" section stated, 'New Orleans Is Not Ready to Think Small, or even Medium.' This article states:

> *"Suggest that New Orleans needs to consider repopulating only elevated areas, leaving flood-prone ones to lie fallow, and you will be shouted down..... Elected officials are not often candid even in the best of times, obviously, but natural disasters create their own warped politics..... Carl Weisbrod, who worked on the Urban Land report and led a business improvement district in Lower Manhattan before and after the Sept. 11 attacks, said, 'There is always for political leaders a fine line to be walked between what the reality is, and how do you mobilize public opinion.'.... 'There are two levels of denial going on here,' said Philip Hart, a real estate executive in California who worked on the Urban Land report. 'One is related to the effects of the natural disaster and the other is denying the fact that the negative perception of Louisiana and New Orleans is hampering the rebuilding process.'"*

In Jed Horne's *Breach of Faith* (2006) account,

> *"As ULI went on with its presentation, it was not hard, through the haze of rhetorical feints and dodges, to see the outlines of a sensible—if politically improbable—plan for*

mitigating future disasters..... The problem that would come with failure to do the redevelopment systematically—concentrating efforts in the most viable areas and restraining it where 'close study' seemed warranted—was the 'jack-o'-lantern syndrome,' the ULI warned. The jack-o'-lantern syndrome—so named because of the gap-toothed look of neighborhoods reviving unevenly—would kick in if you had scattered rebuilding amid widespread abandonment,.... (Oliver)

Thomas began by seeming to reject the ULI analysis. 'Look, the jack-o'-lantern effect is nothing new,' he said. 'There's always been a jack-o'-lantern—for thirty years people have been living with abandoned houses down the block.' But that said, he was willing to throw ULI a rose. 'There are some realities we have to deal with,' he agreed."

On November 28, 2005, Mayor Nagin reiterated his intention to ultimately rebuild all of New Orleans, thus rejecting ULI's strategy for repopulation. On December 13, 2005, Joe Canizaro proposed a three-year plan, which stated that anyone can rebuild anywhere for three years, at which point an inadequate neighborhood in terms of repopulation and the need for the requisite public services, could be shrunk. On December 15, 2005, the City Council passed a resolution that all neighborhoods should get equal treatment and should be rebuilt simultaneously. On January 11, 2006, the BNOB land use committee, chaired by Canizaro, releases and votes to accept its final report calling for a four-month window to allow neighborhoods to prove their viability. On January 21, 2006, Mayor Nagin announces he will not support a moratorium of rebuilding as suggested by the BNOB. On January 27, 2006 the BNOB accepts the final reports from the last six committees, including education, culture, health care, and other matters. On February 20, 2006, Governor Blanco unveils what will become the $7.5 billion Road Home Program, which is approved by the Louisiana Recovery

Authority on March 16, 2006. On March 20, 2006, the BNOB releases its report, with a $12.9 billion price tag for rebuilding the city. On May 20, 2006, Mayor Nagin is re-elected in a delayed election with strong support from African American voters. On May 30, 2006, U.S. Housing and Urban Development Secretary Alphonso Jackson approves the Road Home Program. On June 15, 2006, President Bush signs emergency spending bill for an additional $4.2 billion in Community Development Block Grant (CDBG) funds for Louisiana. On August 22, 2006, Governor Blanco launches the Road Home Program. Three days later on August 25th, the City Council approves the FEMA flood elevation maps. On October 27, 2006, the New Orleans Neighborhoods Rebuilding Plans were unanimously accepted by the City Council.

Moving into December 2006, it was estimated that the city had perhaps 185,000 residents, down from 465,000 pre-Katrina. There was no master plan for rebuilding the city, though small scale plans and individual actions were taking place in certain neighborhoods. But the elected officials, led by Ray Nagin, seemed reluctant to make hard decisions that could introduce some level of rational decision-making both at the macro and micro levels. As Warren Whitlock suggests in his January 2006 *Urban Land* magazine article,

> *"For New Orleans to be rebuilt successfully, the city must first be objective about its past and set a course to build on the best of its heritage. Not doing so may not only be catastrophic for the city's own ability to survive tragedy, but may portend a greater loss for us all."*

Thus, just at the very time that New Orleanians needed to step up and change their insular behavior in order to move forward, the best the city could muster was a 'plan-that-was-not a plan at all.' The political desire to satisfy all those unfortunate individuals and families that had been displaced overwhelmed the need to address reality and try and figure out a strategy that would make a stagnant city a better city in the future.

How did the city reach this point where Ray Nagin became the butt of jokes on late night television and his sometimes off the cuff remarks made for more comedy? In the midst of this maelstrom, Congressman William Jefferson was accused of taking bribes when $90,000 in cash was found in a freezer at his Washington, D.C. residence. Jefferson was then re-elected by his constituency, but at the same time merely reinforced the black eye that plagues New Orleans.

In his Best of 2006 Architecture, Christopher Hawthorne of the *Los Angeles Times* saves 'The Worst' category for New Orleans as he states in the Sunday, December 17, 2006 edition:

> *"No story has been more dispiriting than the continuing lack of progress in New Orleans. Don't believe any reports lamenting the fact that there is no plan in place to guide the post-Katrina reconstruction. The lack of a plan is itself a strategy—and a cynical one at that, orchestrated by developers and political elites to keep the path to future profits uncluttered by the kind of land-use reforms that might protect the city from coming storms."*

Hawthorne's conspiracy theory certainly cedes more intelligence to the development community and political elites in New Orleans than I have experienced since Katrina hit the city. The lack of cooperation between the business community and the political apparatus in that city has been a longstanding problem in forging progress across many aspects of civic life, so to think that such a conspiracy is now in place is hard to believe, however accurately Hawthorne describes what has happened in New Orleans as the worst in urban planning and architecture in the year 2006. However, Hawthorne's analysis reveals a distrust of the power structure in New Orleans to do the right thing.

On a positive note, in late December 2006, Mayor Nagin finally named a recovery czar. The 'master of post-disaster,' urban planner

Edward Blakely, a native of Southern California, and a peripatetic university dean accepted the challenge of trying to plot the recovery road for a city that was sinking fast. Blakely assumed his new position on January 8, 2007, and brings with him a background in developing recovery plans for, Los Angeles after the 1992 Northridge earthquake, the 1989 Loma Prieta earthquake in the San Francisco Bay Area, the Oakland (CA) Hills wildfire in 1991, and with New York City, post 9/11. Clearly, Blakely is bringing a vast reservoir of knowledge to his New Orleans assignment and does not seem to lack for confidence. Yet to be determined is the organizational structure within which Blakely will operate and the degree of autonomy he will have from local politics as he does his work. He will also have to overcome local political dysfunction in New Orleans unseen in his other post-disaster assignments.

I first met Blakely nearly a decade ago when he was Dean of the School of Urban and Regional Planning at the University of Southern California (USC). At the time I was project manager for the building of the 5,000-seat, $60 million West Angeles Cathedral on Crenshaw Boulevard in South Los Angeles. This mega-church has 25,000 members, the vast majority of whom are African American. The West Angeles Cathedral is about 3 miles west of the USC campus on Exposition Boulevard, and at the time was one of the major construction projects along the Crenshaw Corridor, which was still rebuilding after the riots of 1992. Crenshaw Boulevard is a main street through the predominantly African American Crenshaw District, and was a primary route rioters followed after the Rodney King verdict in 1992. By the time I met Blakely there were still scars from this devastating urban riot.

By building this new, vast cathedral, we knew its investment would have an economic impact up and down Crenshaw that is still unfolding. West Angeles Church is now planning the West Angeles Village and West Angeles Cathedral Campus on its 25 plus acres along Crenshaw. I am assisting the church pastor, Bishop Charles

Blake, as Senior Advisor on the building strategy team in our next steps to revitalize this important corridor. This type of faith-based redevelopment of a distressed urban area can be instructive in New Orleans. I have documented this work in my essay 'Building 21st Century Cathedrals in the City of Angels,' which describes the building of West Angeles Cathedral and Our Lady of the Angels Cathedral, the Catholic sanctuary in downtown Los Angeles. This essay details the economic impact and civic role these two large sanctuaries have had in South LA and downtown LA. In a book chapter titled 'A Time to Build,' I discuss the community building ministries of West Angeles Church of God in Christ and First African Methodist Church (FAME), two prominent mega-churches who play central roles in revitalizing the distressed South LA area. This chapter is in the anthology *In the Vineyards: Churches and Community Development (2007)*. My work is reflected in one essential element that ULI identifies as important in spurring rebuilding and long-term viability in New Orleans— that of the role of the faith-based community.

VI

A Failure to Communicate

ULI as the messenger with a message of strategic approaches to rebuilding a city devastated by a hurricane and flooding due to breaches in the levees, understands on their advisory services assignments that the sponsor does not always take their advice. In most of the over 400 such assignments since 1947, a significant number of ULI's recommendations have been accepted and implemented. As noted earlier, New Orleans represents one of the most difficult assignments in the 60-year history of the ULI advisory services program.

Given the unwillingness of key stakeholders in New Orleans to accept ULI's key recommendation regarding a strategy to repopulate the city, what can this failure be attributed to? The lack of acceptance of this key recommendation then had a snowball effect on the city's willingness to accept other of ULI's recommended strategies essential to rebuilding this damaged city. Is it a failure to communicate? Is it in the message? Is it a failure of the messenger?

Perhaps the parting comments of National Hurricane Center Director Max Mayfield, as reported in the *Los Angeles Times* on January 3, 2007, provides some needed perspective.

> *"Frustrated with people and politicians who refuse to listen or learn....Max Mayfield ends his 34-year government career today in search of a new platform for getting out his unwelcome message: Hurricane Katrina was*

nothing compared with the big one yet to come.... What is lacking in the United States is the political will to make and impose hard decisions on building codes and land use in the face of resistance from the influential building industry and a public still willing to gamble that the big one will never hit, he said."

The lack of political will to make and impose hard decisions on land use and the refusal to listen or learn are watchwords relevant to New Orleans. As I think back upon my experience in New Orleans with ULI, BNOB, Ray Nagin and other local elected officials, I think of lack of political will to make hard decisions. I also become frustrated with the inability of the people and politicians in New Orleans to listen and learn. The city still needs to come up with strategies and tactics to repopulate its neighborhoods. I believe that the essence of such an approach will ultimately use the ULI recommendation as a blueprint. If the people and politicians would have been willing to listen and learn in late 2005, and if the politicians would have been able to make hard decisions, then much more progress would have been made in rebuilding this great American city.

There is a logic in collective action as economist Mancur Olson reminded us in his classic book many years ago. ULI rightly noted that in rebuilding New Orleans's neighborhoods, it would take both collective action and individual action. There has been a significant amount of individual action in New Orleans, but it will be collective action that really knits the city back together again and then provides a template for creating an even more vital context within which individuals and groups can grow and thrive. Pre-Katrina was not a New Orleans where individuals and groups could grow and thrive.

The logic of collective action demands leadership on the part of both the public and private sectors. Collective action also implies that there is a macro-oriented plan that guides such action. Political leadership is about building consensus and providing a vision.

Mayor Ray Nagin and the New Orleans City Council have done neither. The only seeming consensus they have reached over the past 18 months is around their dislike of the ULI plan to repopulate the neighborhoods of the city.

The ULI Expert Teams and Advisory Panel came into New Orleans as outsiders where objectivity was needed. The locals did not appreciate their recommendation as to repopulation. The local leadership has chosen to respond to other voices stating the right to return all at once. This subjective interpretation of events is perhaps best understood as a case of 'post traumatic stress syndrome.' It is an emotional response to an emotional situation, but over time if this is the basis of decision-making about how to rebuild, then it will be a very long time before a new New Orleans will rise from the depths of the water that has long receded.

Perhaps one part of the equation around this 'failure to communicate' can also be placed on ULI's shoulders. There is a palpable racial dynamic that was perhaps recognized by ULI in its recommendations, but not truly acknowledged in its subsequent actions. The face of ULI after the panel made its recommendations on November 18, 2005, was principally non-African American. At follow-up meetings in New Orleans and the town hall meetings in other cities such as Atlanta, Houston, etc., the ULI message was being delivered to a predominantly African American audience by a non-African American messenger. As accomplished as is former Pittsburgh, Pennsylvania Mayor Tom Murphy, when he was appointed ULI's liaison to the Gulf Coast, including New Orleans, I knew we had an uphill climb. Similarly, the role of Joseph Canizaro proved problematic in moving forward with the ULI recommendation regarding repopulation of the city. Canizaro played an important role in engaging ULI in this process, but he seems to carry some baggage locally in terms of his true motives.

This difficulty of communicating across the racial divide has a long history, going back to the Atlantic slave trade. Myrdal's 'rank order of discrimination' indeed has relevance today, i.e., black folks and white folks just see things differently and have different ways of communicating with each other as well as across racial lines. I am reminded of one of my acquaintances while in graduate school at Michigan State University in the mid-1960s to the early 1970s. He was black (we were Negro until 1968, at which time we became black). The Lansing State Journal was our local newspaper, and was owned by whites. He used to say that if the State Journal said it was going to rain he would not take an umbrella. If the paper said it was going to be sunny, he would take his umbrella. He understood and expressed Myrdal's rank order of discrimination in his own personal way.

Similarly, ULI made a tactical mistake when it did not fully understand the need for the messenger to be more in tune with the message and the audience. A city that is 2/3 African American is going to respond with distrust and alienation when the message is being delivered by a non-African American messenger. In our meetings in New Orleans over the period from November 12-18th, I tried to convey this message to my fellow panel members and ULI leadership. I do not think my message was fully understood.

It seems to be a matter of my Michigan State University colleague's attitude, i.e., if Joe Canizaro recommends a certain way to proceed, then the African American stakeholders will reject it out of hand. If ULI and its non-African American representatives state a certain position, then the African American stakeholders will take an opposing view. If this is indeed the case, it is truly an American dilemma, for in the midst of one of the worst natural and man-made disasters in the nation's history, important questions of rebuilding are being held hostage by the racial divide.

Interpersonal communication is categorized as being either verbal, non-verbal or symbolic. An unfortunate example of symbolic communication was when Ray Nagin did not attend the ULI presentation of its recommendations on November 18, 2005. He was in Washington, D.C. pressing his case for federal support of his city, which was necessary and admirable. At the same time, federal officials were pressing him to come up with a responsible plan to rebuild the city. The symbolism of Nagin not being present at the ULI presentation bothers me to this day.

Again, going back to classical sociology, the literature of contemporary social science advances two models for interpreting the exercise of social power in issue resolution within American society. Both models, the negative and the positive, stress the importance of large-scale organizations. The negative power model envisions power manipulations, which benefit particular groups, which is an anti-synergistic conception. Thus Christopher Hawthorne's view as recently expressed in the *Los Angeles Times* that the lack of a plan to rebuild in New Orleans is merely a cynical strategy orchestrated by developers and political elites is an example of a negative power model.

Large-scale organizations are unique social inventions; and the problem for any society is that of planning its organizations so that desired goals are achieved. To have designed the organizational structure necessary to produce knowledge and technology, that has affected the behavior of so many millions of people, represents positive power over the decision making of human behavior.

Consensus is the congruence of preferences of the affected units, and in voluntaristic theories is viewed as open to manipulation by charismatic leadership and/or mass media. There is generally a trade-off between consensus and control; that is the more consensus, the less need for control, and the less consensus, the more need for control.

How does this sociological jargon relate to rebuilding New Orleans and a failure to communicate? Seemingly, a negative power model is extant in New Orleans rather than a positive model of power. In addition, I would not categorize Ray Nagin as a charismatic leader.

Further, there is a critical need to build consensus around strategies to rebuild New Orleans in order to move this process forward. In so doing, collective action is needed as a tool of societal guidance in concert with individual action.

Finally, as a large-scale organization, what are the rebuilding goals for the City of New Orleans? Seemingly, the right of return is a goal of both the Mayor and City Council. How can this worthy goal best be achieved? Another goal seems to be an emphasis on individual action over the logic of collective action. This is expressed by the Mayor's stated goal of allowing rebuilding to take place in every neighborhood of the city despite the level of destruction, toxicity, or the city's ability to provide public services. What is the city's goal as to the footprint of the city in 5, 10, 15 or 20 years out? What is the organizational structure that can best carry out the city's rebuilding goals? Is it the already existing planning and redevelopment apparatus now in place? What are the city's goals in terms of rebuilding and strengthening the infrastructure, including the levees?

In the absence of a charismatic leader, and with the lack of consensus, along with the seeming dominance of a negative power model, a need for more control is suggested. Where will such control emanate? Will it be top-down or bottom-up? New Orleans seems to be the city that is governed by a bottom-up perspective, thus an over-emphasis on individual action as opposed to collective action. In this context, perhaps it is asking too much for ULI and others to expect that a rebuilding strategy that calls for a combination of collective action and individual action would find traction in New Orleans.

Granted, ULI has a long history of conducting advisory service panels with cities and towns, universities, and other nonprofit and for-profit organizations, including a number of panels in New Orleans itself. But even with the extensive investment made by ULI in New Orleans, its basic recommendation for repopulation seems to have been held hostage by the racial divide and communication confusion.

The introduction of recovery czar Edward Blakely into this volatile mix stands to be a good thing. Blakely is a highly regarded urban planner who is African American and carries a high regard for the Urban Land Institute (ULI). He is also sensitive to the unique history and culture of New Orleans as well as being politically astute. He is capable of communicating across the racial divide and within the African American class structure. After months of pessimism in observing how New Orleans was addressing its planning and rebuilding challenges, the appointment of Blakely offers one glimmer of hope for this city under siege. How much autonomy and control will Blakely have as the recovery czar? That is the $64 billion question.

The study of communication concerns itself with the acts of humans, which affect the decisions of other humans. For example, the final report of a project, such as the ULI report to the Bring New Orleans Back Commission, is a message intended to modify or justify a course of action pursued by leadership in a purposeful state. The value of the report may be due to either the disclosure of a new alternative course of action or the demonstration of greater effectiveness of a course of action known to, but not currently used by the leadership. In either case, if the leadership's policy is changed because of the disclosure or demonstration, information has been transmitted.

It is commonly recognized that when the recommendations contained in most reports are accepted a critical step still remains, that of implementation. Implementation is problematic because the recommended course of action may be followed with varying degrees of efficiency. Implementation in New Orleans remains problematic. The level of efficiency in following a course of action that is consistent with the city's rebuilding goals has been very low. Blakely's challenge in working with the city's elites and non-elites will be to build consensus around rebuilding goals which can be implemented with a high level of efficiency.

VII

Minority Developers and New Orleans

Background

When Hurricane Katrina hit the Gulf Coast and the city of New Orleans, Louisiana on August 29, 2005, it left in its aftermath the most destructive and costliest natural disaster in U.S. history. In addition to the estimated damage of $200 billion to $300 billion, there were more than one million people displaced, thus creating a humanitarian crisis on a scale not seen in the United States since the Great Depression.

Over twelve months later, the city of New Orleans remains at a crossroads.

Prior experience has suggested that it is essential to develop a redevelopment plan within the first 90 to 120 days following a disaster—whether man-made or natural. As noted in the ULI report "New Orleans, Louisiana: A Strategy for Rebuilding," the failure to create an immediate and forward-thinking plan can result in scattered, uncoordinated, dysfunctional redevelopment; an ineffective infrastructure policy; and a greatly impaired urban fabric.

But as a June 18, 2006 *New York Times* headline notes, "In New Orleans, Money Is Ready But a Plan Isn't." This article goes on to state that local officials have yet to come up with a redevelopment plan showing what kind of city will emerge from the storm's ruins.

New Orleans was a city of 465,000 pre-Katrina, of which nearly two-thirds were African-American. The issues of the city's post-Katrina footprint and its impact on the racial makeup of the city in the storm's aftermath are two of the stumbling blocks in formulating a plan that can gain consensus.

Pre-Katrina in the city of New Orleans' nearly one in three African Americans lived below the poverty line. Thus despite having African American mayors governing the city since 1978, much work remained in order to bring this racial group into the economic mainstream. Included in this disparity is the paucity of African American real estate developers and building contractors available to fully participate in rebuilding the Crescent City. Thus the question: 'Is there a role for minority developers in the rebuilding of New Orleans?'

Small Business: The Backbone of the Community

- Among the key findings and recommendations of the ULI New Orleans report that relate to the issue of small business are the following:

- Diversity, equity and cooperation are of critical importance. The recovery must not be held back by the racial issues that have slowed progress in the past.

- Planning for the rebuilding of each neighborhood must involve the citizens from that neighborhood.

- The city needs diverse economic development and housing. Jobs and housing will be the backbone of the city's rebirth.

- Business leadership must work in partnership with government.

- A diversified economic development strategy that takes into account and builds upon those businesses and industries present prior to Katrina, as well as those that may be appropriate in a renewed city, is critical to the city's redevelopment.

- The city should be rebuilt in a strategic manner.

- People who cannot rebuild should be given fair compensation for their property.

Small business is the backbone of the U.S. economy, and perhaps more so in New Orleans than in most major metropolitan areas. For even before Katrina, New Orleans was not a city of big corporations. Rather it was a city of mom-and-pop groceries, family-owned barbecue joints, lawyers who hung out a shingle instead of joining a big firm, and bar owners who knew their customers by name. Of the 22,000 businesses in Orleans Parish before the August 2005 storm, 21,000 of these had fewer than 99 employees.

Small businesses were devastated by Hurricane Katrina. This includes minority owned real estate development companies as well as those in the building trades businesses. In the short-term, in order to get back on their feet in order to compete for the billions of dollars in federal, state and private dollars that are flowing into the city for rebuilding purposes, these developers need what most other small businesses require in this daunting situation. These needs include

access to capital. The ULI panel in its report recommended that small business programs offering financial assistance should include the following: loan and grant funding; partial government guarantees of small business loans to private sector lenders; flexible use of proceeds; use of existing infrastructure to expedite delivery of these dollars; streamlined application process; and nontaxable government grants. Other recommended short term actions included technical assistance and other non-monetary support.

As to the long-term, the ULI panel recommended the following. That an investment fund be created to mobilize the business community to help rebuild the local economy. This fund should invest in local businesses, with a particular focus on minority-owned companies, and in other economic development projects. This fund should provide both debt and equity and be an evergreen fund whose returns would be reinvested in other businesses.

Further, the process of rebuilding New Orleans will be a major source of economic activity and growth for the city. Other parts of the country have seen this process of rebuilding and growth after natural disasters. However, if specific steps are not taken much of the planning and physical construction will likely be carried out by national and regional companies that do not have much local presence. This is indeed what is occurring in New Orleans.

As the physical rebuilding of New Orleans is unfolding low income city residents either remain displaced, or they have been relegated to the low-wage jobs that offer little opportunity for career growth. One benefit of employing local residents is that the multiplier effect is likely to be greater than that employing non-local workers.

The physical rebuilding of New Orleans is going to require the combined skills of planners, architects, engineers, real estate developers, construction managers, building contractors, the labor force, and stakeholders throughout the city, along with lots of money—from both the public and private sectors. It is of course unrealistic to expect that the proportion of federal dollars flowing into the city will be distributed to the African American business community anywhere near their pre-Katrina percentage of the city's population. Given this reality, what is possible in terms of a real role for minority developers and other land use professionals in the rebuilding of New Orleans?

From Crisis to Opportunity?

Often out of crisis comes opportunity. New Orleans has been in a crisis now for over a year since the force of Hurricane Katrina turned the city upside down. As has been amply noted elsewhere, New Orleans had been declining even before Katrina blew into town. Is it possible for this crippled city to take advantage of the opportunity before it to reshape the city so as to become a newer, better place, yet rooted in its historic strengths? Is it possible for minority developers and builders to secure their fair share of the dollars set to flow into the Crescent City in this redevelopment process? Are there viable examples of minority developers carving out a piece of the action in redevelopment projects elsewhere that can be replicated in New Orleans?

Given the integral relationship between housing and jobs in the creation of a community, an important immediate opportunity in New Orleans for minority developers is with producing housing stock for as people return there is a workforce for local businesses. As noted in a recent ULI New Orleans housing proposal, the fundamental question for the people of New Orleans is "How can I rebuild?" The ULI plan done in conjunction with the Bring New Orleans Back Housing Subcommittee and the New Orleans Neighborhood Development Collaborative, combines public and private funds to rebuild 74,000 owner-occupied homes and 47,500 low-income and workforce rental units. This plan provides the options needed to begin to rebuild neighborhoods by creating housing for over 300,000 residents.

The question of available labor is also relevant to the rebuilding process. To this end, in late July 2006 the Business Roundtable, an association of 160 chief executives of major companies, launched an effort to recruit and train as many as 20,000 new construction workers for the Gulf Coast region. This amid a desperate shortage of labor to rebuild the Gulf Coast, including New Orleans.

The goal of this housing production plan is to encourage home-owners to return to New Orleans by developing financing tools to provide all impacted homeowners with options to rebuild their home in place where appropriate. The plan also offers homeowners that cannot rebuild in place the option to sell their home and provide them with incentives to build or buy a new home in Orleans Parish. Further, the plan seeks to create opportunities to turn 10,000 renters into first-time homeowners. In total, an esti-mated 185,000 residents can be provided with housing using this plan.

Among the 64,000 flooded owner-occupied homes in New Orleans, 52,000 were inside the flood plain. Of the flooded owner-occupied homes, 40,000 had flood and hazard insurance, with 35,000 of these within the flood plain. Those owner-occupied homes without flood insurance numbered 24,000, with 17,000 of these falling within the flood plain.

The ULI plan estimates a price tag of $3.0 billion to $3.7 billion funded through federal Community Development Block Grant (CDBG) funds and loans to rebuild housing whether within or outside the flood plain. The plan estimates a total cost of $1.0 billion to build housing for first time homebuyers from sources such as CDBG grants and tax exempt bonds. As to rental housing, the goal of the plan is to provide incentives to landlords to rebuild 47,500 units. Of the rental units created, 24,000 will serve low income renters and 23,500 will provide workforce housing. In total, the plan estimates that 118,750 residents will be provided with affordable housing.

This plan identifies housing types to be produced as being; homeowners; low income renters; workforce renters; first-time home-owners; and special needs renters. The housing finance for this production by source of funds is; Section 8; Hope VI; tax exempt bonds; CDBG; insurance; and new private investment. These housing proposals build on the set of recommendations made in the ULI New Orleans report which is based upon the premise that New Orleans's property owners are entitled to fair compensation and equitable rede-velopment opportunities that provide sufficient resources to rebuild in place or rebuild in developable areas of the city.

With these billions in housing funds in the pipeline, along with the billions needed in public and private dollars to rebuild public schools, commercial properties, YMCAs, churches, shopping centers, and other physical structures, there are clearly ample opportunities for real estate developers citywide. How do minority developers get a piece of this pie? Currently there is no plan in place to guide the redevelopment process, nor is there a plan to bring minority developers into the main-stream to take advantage of this opportunity.

A July 7, 2006 *Boston Globe* article "Flawed solutions in New Orleans," states that it is City Hall's decision to minimize govern-ment meddling in the recovery and rely instead on the magic of the market to allocate Washington's billions and shape the 'new New Orleans.' This laissez-faire approach will ultimately lead to a 'new

New Orleans' coming about via decisions largely made by the insurance industry.

Such a market-based approach will also do no favors for minority developers who will find themselves on the outside looking in as billions are spent to rebuild their city by national and regional real estate development firms. Past history suggests that a proactive stance by government and other stakeholders is needed in order for minority developers to play a real role in redevelopment opportunities. In "Boston's Parcel to Parcel Linkage Plan" *Urban Land*, July 2005) an innovative plan is described whereby minority developers played a prominent role in the building of a 36-story, one million plus square foot office tower in Boston's Financial District, which not only created wealth but also threw off considerable community benefits for needy neighborhoods. This office tower was built for $350 million and was sold for a record $705 million in early 2005, less than eighteen months after completion.

A similar plan is needed in New Orleans, only on a much larger scale. Currently Mayor Ray Nagin, members of the New Orleans City Council, and other local elected officials, earn a failing grade in their diligence in addressing the difficult rebuilding questions facing this city. One year after Katrina destroyed the city little progress has been made in translating the ULI strategies for rebuilding into a plan with consensus that can guide the redevelopment process. Crises often bring leadership to the fore in ways not seen before. We have yet to see this type of leadership rise to the top in New Orleans. One tangible way to try to regain the high ground is for public sector officials at city, state and federal levels to be proactive in demanding that minority developers and related land use professionals get their fair share of the billions to be spent in rebuilding New Orleans, whatever the footprint looks like. In addition, there are still difficult decisions to be made as to strategies for rebuilding and re-populating the neighborhoods, in a city of neighborhoods.

With the billions of dollars available for redevelopment projects throughout the city of New Orleans, this will attract motivated developers and other land use professionals who want to get a piece of this substantial pie. In this context, Mayor Nagin should complement his use of the bully pulpit with an awareness that with billions at stake he can guide motivated developers to make sure they do the right thing. In addition, part of his agenda should be to guide a chunk of these billions to local black banks which have been adversely effected by Katrina's aftermath.

The other side of this coin is whether the minority development community in New Orleans has the capacity and capability to participate fully in a multi-billion dollar rebuilding program. In Boston, this capacity and capability question was answered through the use of partnerships and joint ventures. It is incumbent upon the national and regional developers to actively look to partner with smaller minority development companies. So too can President George Bush be proactive in this regard as most of the billions to be spent in New Orleans will be federal dollars. President Bush can keep his word delivered on September 15, 2005 at New Orleans's Jackson Square when he stated, "I also offer this pledge of the American people: Throughout the area hit by the hurricane, we will do what it takes, we will stay as long as it takes, to help citizens rebuild their communities and their lives." It is incumbent upon all parties interested in the life and not the death of a great American city to make sure President Bush's words are made real.

This article is based upon Hart's remarks at the 9th Annual African American Business Summit in Palm Springs, CA on June 22, 2006.

Reprinted with permission of ULI-Urban Land Institute, Washington, DC.

PORCH**TALK**

Heard they were watching deals go down without a piece
Of the action that's rightly theirs on deals downtown
Sure enough minority contractors are more than decent

Right, they need attorneys and techs to get some relief
Elected leaders need to reach out with programs
Yeah, they were watching deals go down without a piece

Gentlemen, Katrina tore what they built for sale and lease
Oil company derricks were flying through the rain
Sure enough minority contractors are more than decent

Ladies, the storm of architects also didn't please us
Urbanists pushed porches and postmodernists wouldn't
When emotions subside will they deal these guys a piece?

Unless like before they can't get the public to believe
They're entitled to help without lawyers and techs
Sure enough minority contractors are more than decent

Pray to God Katrina will stimulate a new outreach
To get some small entrepreneurs-based programs
You know they watched deals go down without a piece
Sure enough minority contractors work more than decent

ED ROSENTHAL is a poet/commercial real estate broker in the Los Angeles downtown
arts district. He writes poetry primarily dedicated to real estate.

VIII

A Reasonable Blueprint

There is still a need in New Orleans to come up with both a collective and individual action plan to repopulate the neighborhoods. Simultaneously, the levees need to be rebuilt to at least Category 3 strength in the short run and Category 5 strength in the long run. Concurrent to the levees being rebuilt, the citizens of New Orleans, both in the city and displaced with hope of returning to the city, need to be assured that the levees have been designed and constructed in a safe fashion, and that they will be maintained to a higher degree than pre-Katrina. The public schools need to be rebuilt and made into quality institutions to serve the school age population in the city as they have not done in the past. The economy needs to be diversified, building on the strength of the existing pre-Katrina economy and building upon that to create jobs that pay better than the tourism industry and that have clear career paths. City government needs to become more effective and efficient as never before. Of course, housing of all types needs to be built, including workforce housing.

How is this laundry list of rebuilding tasks to be accomplished? This is in essence the same list that existed when ULI first got involved in New Orleans in October 2005. There is still the need for a blueprint to guide the rebuilding process. The ULI blueprint as provided to BNOB is still the only game in town. The one area of major disagreement with this blueprint was around the notion of how to repopulate the neighborhoods. The balance of the ULI recommendations relating to the levees, the economy, culture, government effectiveness, and housing, all still have relevance. Even the ULI repopulation strategy has relevance, though local politics and the racial divide rendered it a eunuch of sorts.

In addition to this list of rebuilding tasks facing the city, that old standby of public safety is still begging for a plan of action to make New Orleans a safe city. Remember, in the summer of 2005 right before Hurricane Katrina blew into town, New Orleans was declared the most dangerous city in the nation. Crime and violence abated with Katrina and the subsequent evacuation of the city. However, as of early 2007 public safety was again on everyone's mind. Between December 28, 2006 and January 7, 2007, twelve people were killed in the city. One victim was a teacher and drummer for the Hot 8 Brass Band. Another victim was an independent filmmaker who was killed at her home as her physician husband was shot three times in front of their two-year old son.

Stella Baty Landis knew these two victims and stated at the time that this was the first time she felt scared to live in New Orleans. Landis who teaches music at Tulane University and is the proprietor of a coffee shop in the city's Lower Marigny neighborhood describes the city as a 'war zone.' Landis also said she does not feel the city's elected officials have focused their attention on the escalating spate of crime and murders. Mayor Nagin has described most of the crime as being 'black on black' and 'it's unfortunate.'

Rev. John C. Raphael, Jr., who in early January 2007 staged a three-day fast to protest the crime in his Central City neighborhood stated that witnesses to crimes are reluctant to come forward because of distrust of the police. He also expressed disappointment over the lack of community action and any sort of united response to the rise in crime. In addition to Rev. Raphael, many community activists believe city officials are in denial about the crime in their city. Landis feels that the city officials are fearful of scaring people off—tourists, potential investors—so is reluctant to publicize anything negative about the city. Landis and other residents of the city said the latest spate of violent crimes in late 2006 and early 2007 and the seeming inability of authorities to stamp it out has made them re-think whether to remain in New Orleans.

As usual, officials of the New Orleans Metropolitan Convention and Visitors Bureau were advising its clients, including convention organizers and tour operators, that the violence was confined to areas where tourists do not typically go. According to J. Stephen Perry, President and CEO of the Convention and Visitors Bureau, in a statement made in January 2007, the city has one of the lowest rates of crime on visitors and tourists, compared to other cities. However, if you have ever visited New Orleans, you realize it's not that distant from the center of tourism activities downtown and 'dangerous' neighborhoods.

How does the city move forward? How can the existing individual actions inspire collective action such that the city can overcome the obstacles in its path? Can a collective spirit arise that has the whole city as the objective of rebirth, rather than just my house or my neighborhood? What will it take to forge a higher vision?

As a guide to trying to answer these questions and to come up with a reasonable blueprint for rebuilding the city, let's visit one neighborhood. Let's also visit the current progress in rebuilding safe and secure levees that can inspire confidence in the city among those wishing to return as well as the insurance industry and investors.

In a December 25, 2006 front-page article in the *Los Angeles Times* titled 'Memories fill the void on a block in New Orleans,' the tale of one neighborhood reveals the emotions and complexities associated with the rebuilding endeavor.

> *"For blacks in New Orleans at the height of Jim Crow, there were few aspirations higher than owning one of the modest brick bungalows in Pontchartrain Park. When the postal workers and teachers and longshoremen wrote*

their last rent checks and moved into the newly developed subdivision, they crossed a portal directly into the middle class....Today, nearly 16 months after Hurricane Katrina submerged the neighborhood up to its rooflines, the Johnsons are the only residents back on their once-bustling block. As they wait for federal grants and rebuild-ing loans, 80-year old Thomas (Johnson), 56-year old Cherrylane and her 22-year old daughter, Taiese, reside in a pair of claustrophobic Federal Emergency Management Agency trailers in the frontyard of a now-darkened cul-de-sac....This is how New Orleans' most devastated neighborhoods are being reclaimed—one house at a time, a few on this block, perhaps none on the next, the resettle-ment driven by market forces with little government intervention. Despite the risk of future flooding, those returning to Pontchartrain Park want it this way."

This is the jack-o-lantern effect that ULI warned about in its recommendations. However, at the individual level the jack-o-lantern effect seems to be alright with those intent on rebuilding their homes and their lives. But is it alright for a city to encourage such an approach to rebuilding without a concurrent collective rebuilding action plan? The notion of resettlement being driven by market forces with little government intervention sounds like a conservative Republican dream come true, but does not seem consistent with a progressive Democratic approach to the role of government.

What about progress on rebuilding the levees as we move toward hurricane season number two following the hurricane season that brought Katrina to New Orleans? As reported in the *Los Angeles Times* on Sunday, December 31, 2006 in an article titled 'New Orleans levee-risk study faulted,'

"When the Army Corps of Engineers admitted in June (2006) that design flaws in the New Orleans levee system

had caused most of the flooding during Hurricane Katrina, it seemingly left little to argue about. But the fight wasn't over. The Corps is now engaged in an effort to predict how New Orleans would fare in the next big hurricane, and is once again being second-guessed by some of the nation's top civil engineers..... 'Is it acceptable to have the worst natural disaster in U.S. history occur over and over again?' asked David Daniel, president of the University of Texas at Dallas and the leader of the American Society of Civil Engineers team that is reviewing the Corps' Katrina investigation. 'I don't think it is.' 'Until the banking and insurance industries believe the risks are tolerable, you are not going to see much building going on in New Orleans,' Daniel said. 'They understand risk as well as anybody.'"

Couple these two pictures of jack-o-lantern rebuilding neighborhood by neighborhood with the lack of certainty in levee reconstruction with the outcomes of a recent ULI Study Tour to the Gulf Coast that included New Orleans, and one comes away with a pessimistic view of the future for this city unless a reasonable blueprint can find life. On this ULI Study Tour, a group of thirty investors and developers toured New Orleans and the Gulf Coast. In New Orleans, this group stated they saw neither a plan nor anyone who was in charge of rebuilding the city. They expressed doubt about investing in the city as they could not comfortably identify an exit strategy. Whether we like it or not, investors and real estate developers create projects and the resultant pro formas based on a reasonable exit strategy and a reasonable return on investment. One good note of news in all of this talk of exit strategies and return on investment is that in late December of 2006, a San Diego-based investment firm bought a downtown New Orleans high-rise, the first sale of a major office building in the city since Hurricane Katrina struck in 2005. Equastone, which specializes in buying, fixing up and leasing or selling commercial properties in growth and recovery markets, paid about $50 million for the 28-story Pan-American Life Insurance Company building. This deal came at a time when the city, still feeling the effects of the storm, was eager for new investment.

This bit of good news in the commercial property sector which is a 'high ground' transaction is meaningful, but not quite the great news that the city needs in terms of the below sea level neighborhoods. For months now, New Orleans has had a plan to develop a plan starting with the ULI-BNOB process beginning in October 2005. The Ford Foundation has granted the city nearly $3.0 million for a neighborhood planning process that is to bring all of New Orleans under the same umbrella of a rational plan. In a July 11, 2006 interview with National Public Radio (NPR), *New Orleans Times Picayune* reporter Jed Horne states that the neighborhoods on their own initiative have undertaken their own kinds of neighborhood assessment and formulated their own kinds of wish lists and plans for rebuilding. Horne references the Broadmoor section of town as doing some good thinking at the neighborhood level as to planning. Horne goes on to note in this NPR interview that despite the good example of neighborhoods such as Broadmoor, the city and region need to be re-thought because you cannot build transit in individual neighborhoods. It has to cross neighborhoods and reach out beyond the city limits themselves—and you have to rethink the ways in which in some cases the transit tracks with proper installation might double as an interior levee system, as ULI proposed. This ULI proposal, which was endorsed by the BNOB, would have light rail transit tracks on a raised bed. Such a light rail system could link the city together from east to west and span out to the airport and eventually to Baton Rouge.

The tracks could be raised on an earthen mound leading to the creation of interior basins that if a levee breach were to occur in the future, you would not have the entire city being flooded; you would just have that quadrant of that portion of the city possibly flooding, which would be far better than the case after Katrina. This light rail transit plan was criticized in certain quarters as they seemingly did not understand the role such a system could play in flood prevention as well as in evacuation after flooding. In addition, Horne's concern is that such a plan will not see the light of day as it is jeopardized by the willy-nilly decision to let people rebuild wherever they will, wherever they once were, rather than retrenching to a consolidated city then letting that city grow back, if it in fact retains and recovers the economic vigor to warrant growing back to its old footprint.

It was on January 21, 2006 that Mayor Nagin announced he will not support a moratorium on rebuilding as recommended by the BNOB. This was just five days after Nagin made his infamous 'Chocolate City' and 'Vengeful God' speech on Martin Luther King, Jr. Day. Earlier that same month on January 1, it was duly documented that Mayor Nagin's city was now the third largest city in Louisiana after Baton Rouge and Shreveport with a population of 135,000. Nagin's decision to promote rebuilding throughout the city basically aborted any potential for long-term planning that could perhaps put New Orleans on a path for growth and prosperity. It was a short-term decision with an eye toward his re-election.

The *Times Picayune* in a June 11, 2006 article 'Developers are Building Skyward as a Solution to New Orleans Post-Katrina Housing Shortage,' states that developers are proposing high-rise residential complexes downtown and are not facing the resistance they faced before the storm. City Planning Commission executive Yolanda Rodriquez said at the time that pre-Katrina, density was a dirty word in New Orleans. This wave of new high-rise proposals could become one of the biggest trends in post-Katrina New Orleans. The projects in the pipeline could more than double the number of high-rise residential units from 2,100 to 4,300. As in other cities such as Los Angeles, a number of the projects involve the conversion of existing office buildings into residential complexes. Doris Koo of Enterprise Community Investment Partners notes that density with the right design that is respectful of the neighborhood character is a good and efficient way of restoring housing as quickly as possible in New Orleans. But Koo stressed the three elements that can make such projects successful: the right income mix, the right social services and the right areas.

There are a number of reasons for the spate of proposed high-rise residential developments in New Orleans. One reason is the Gulf Coast Opportunity Zone Act, which offers incentives, especially increases in historic tax credits for buildings that are 50 or more years old. The amount of low-income tax credits available in the state has also increased in the Gulf Opportunity Zone—up to $65 million in 2006 compared to $8.5 million in 2005. Both ULI and the American Institute of Architects (AIA) recommended upper-floor living on Canal Street and in vertical towers as the city endeavored to stay within the confines of higher ground. One real estate developer involved with one of these high-rise projects, Roth Walsh, stated that there is a reason that Bienville settled the French Quarter where he did—it was on high ground.

Another reason that high-rise residential units are gaining new traction in high ground neighborhoods in the city relates to the updated construction codes, which means that newly constructed buildings are better able to withstand wind and flooding, and as a result, better able to attract the city's returning population. Downtown structures built since 2000 fared better during Katrina than office towers that were built in the 1980s. Several developers have stated that downtown New Orleans needs to become more vertical. High-rise apartment units may be even more in demand than high-rise condominiums because displaced residents need housing immediately and are more likely to gravitate toward apartments. In addition, the fact that buildings qualifying for historic tax credits must remain rentals for five years means developers will be partial to building rental units as opposed to for sale condominium units.

As noted in the Times Picayune article 'high-rise' can be somewhat of a misnomer in New Orleans. In most cities, structures that are 20 stories or more qualify as high-rises. But in New Orleans—its preference for two-and-three-story 19th century commercial corridors—a 12-to-15-story building is usually called a high-rise. The wave of projects on the drawing board promises to change the face of New Orleans by introducing more urban living. Such high-rise development in concert with a light rail vehicle transit system would put New Orleans in line with current smart growth thinking with its transit oriented development (TOD) thinking. If this transit can be designed as an additional levee protection system as recommended by ULI, New Orleans would make huge strides in terms of sustainability.

However, it is quite clear that New Orleans has lagged behind other cities in the nation and the world in terms of vertical living. Peter Trapolin, a New Orleans preservationist, notes that the new mid-rise and high-rise complexes provide the city an opportunity to develop urban options as well as accompanying neighborhood retail sites. Trapolin goes on to note that it is the density and urban living that makes an urban corridor work.

As to corridor planning, two recent ULI advisory panels that I served on may be instructive in relationship to New Orleans. Earlier I had mentioned the Camden, New Jersey ULI panel I served on in June 2004 (Camden was 'recognized' as the most dangerous city in the nation in 2004 and was succeeded in this 'honor' by New Orleans in 2005). We were asked in Camden to provide recommendations as to the market potential, planning and design issues, development strategies and implementation for the Haddon Avenue Corridor. This distressed urban corridor connects two medical facilities which bookend a community marked by jack-o-lantern housing and commercial space. The ULI panel was asked by the City of Camden to provide a strategy for strengthening this corridor, and thus the surrounding neighborhoods.

In the conclusion of the Camden, New Jersey report published in 2004, the panel states that the Historic Haddon Avenue corridor should be redeveloped with a vision that recognizes both the importance of the health care community and the rich history of the neighborhoods that surround it. The vision needs to honor Haddon Avenue's legacy as a special place. This is a colonially platted community that joined with the elegant new residential area along the Cooper River in the early 1900s. It is a place where the past has always merged with the future.

The panel recommends targeting three distinct locations along Historic Haddon Avenue for concentrated redevelopment. Entries into the neighborhood should be redesigned as passages that convey history and pride in the local community. Haddon Passage can be linked with the Cooper University Hospital complex and redeveloped as a mixed-use area sensitive to the existing scale of buildings along both sides of the passage. A landmark image can be developed at Haddon Square, an area that eventually should become the heart of the community. In June 2004 when the ULI panel was in Camden, this location was the site of a donut shop where it is alleged that extensive illegal drug activity was centered. The transit oriented development (TOD) planned at the Ferry Avenue PATCO station across from Our Lady of Lourdes Medical Center should be linked with the corridor and should help create a pedestrian environment that is safe and attractive.

Stakeholders must continue to work together to promote the revitalization of the avenue and the development of a retail core. Cooperation among the neighborhoods of Parkside, Whitman Park, and Gateway will be crucial to the success of the area's redevelopment. This success will build upon Haddon Avenue's existing strengths: a distinctive history, an impressive stock of early 20th century architecture, its pedestrian scale, and the potential for a dynamic retail and entertainment mix not found elsewhere in Camden. In reviewing the panel's recommendations for Camden, I can see several similarities between strategies to rebuild New Orleans and Camden—thus giving me hope that perhaps in the not too distant future both these distressed cities can be known for more than being America's most dangerous cities.

In November 2004 I served on another ULI advisory panel in San Antonio, Texas. Similar to Camden, New Jersey, this panel was asked to make recommendations to revitalize the East Commerce Street Corridor. In our subsequent report "St. Paul Gateway District: San Antonio, Texas," issued in 2005, the panel concluded that four framing statements best articulate the need for redevelopment along this corridor. These framing statements are:

- Reconnecting with the city
- Humanizing the corridor
- Investing in the district; and
- Establishing a new focus and a new identity.

The panel renamed the East Commerce Street corridor study area, calling it the St. Paul Gateway District. Because the area is plagued by negative perceptions caused primarily by conditions of neglect, it was agreed that a new name would perhaps help establish a new identity for the area. The goal of the panel's proposed redevelopment plan is to build upon the area's historic and cultural resources and create a mixed-income residential community characterized by its arts and entertainment venues as well as its historic characteristics. As more people choose to live closer to downtown, this area just east of downtown can provide an ideal location for the development of mixed-price housing, new businesses, and accompanying employment opportunities within a district known for its unique identity.

Both the city of Camden and the St. Paul neighborhood in San Antonio have predominantly African American populations. Like New Orleans, both Camden and San Antonio have unique identities rooted in African American culture that can be turned into assets. In both Camden and San Antonio, corridor redevelopment strategies were emphasized as a way to promote redevelopment and a new identity.

Can such a strategy find a footing in New Orleans? As local developer Pres Kabacoff writes in *Urban Land* magazine in January 2006;

> *"Before Hurricane Katrina, I was among a number of individuals who proposed Operation Rebirth, a road map for reinvigorating the city. We recommended taking 4,000 acres comprising 14 downtown neighborhoods on both sides of the Mississippi River, then identifying public/private partnership development opportunities to fill the empty spaces in those communities. An essential part of the plan was to revitalize Canal Street, the city's major artery. One recommendation was to create the Louisiana Music Experience in an abandoned theater on the upper end of the street. The city's rich music history is a significant cultural asset, but unlike Nashville, we have not made it an industry....Operation Rebirth also recommended that Oretha Castle Haley Boulevard, an important center-city street, be developed as an African American cultural and entertainment district....Also part of the 4,000 acres designated for redevelopment was the medical district, which employs 30,000 people. Development there should be continued and include biotech facilities and a cancer research center....We have an opportunity to extend streetcar service up and down the river, connecting the industrial canal to the Lower Garden District, and ultimately, expanding the streetcar lines in the central part of the city."*

Clearly, some thought has been given to a corridor redevelopment strategy in New Orleans pre-Katrina. In this post-Katrina redevelopment environment, it probably makes even more sense to utilize such a strategy. Of course, a corridor implies streets. What makes for a great street? In January 2006, I served on another ULI advisory panel in Washington, D.C., where that was the essence of our assignment. In the 2006 ULI report titled "Great Street: Washington, D.C.—A Strategy for Implementation," it is noted that the intent of the Great Streets program is to revitalize corridors along their entire length rather than a specific district or node and to improve the communities that border them. The six Great Streets corridors were recognized not only as being critical in the District of Columbia, but also as being in areas with strong local organizations and leaders capable of partnering with public agencies to encourage 'clean and safe' activities and to program public events and activities that use in a positive way the enhanced public spaces. The communities along the Great Streets are also working communities whose diverse neighborhoods are beginning to grow after a long period of disinvestment.

The ULI Great Streets panel included lectures and case studies from around the world. This thinking can be instructive for New Orleans in its efforts to rebuild great streets as well. Allan Jacobs, author of Great Streets, and former planning director of San Francisco, gave a presentation on the key elements that make up Great Streets for the ULI panel and key Washington, D.C. city officials and stakeholders. In addition, Jacobs shared examples of Great Streets from around the world.

ULI panelists also presented case studies of corridor revitalization projects in various stages of completion from around the country. The projects included Indiana Avenue in Indianapolis, Indiana; High Street in Columbus, Ohio; the Pearl District in Portland, Oregon; and Washington Street in Boston, Massachusetts. The case studies explained the planning process for creating Great Streets, detailed the complex partnerships that were formed to create change, and shared their success stories and lessons learned.

What makes for a Great Street? As the ULI report states, streets are more than transportation and infrastructure. They are the place where private property meets the public realm. This interface must delicately balance a multitude of essential sectors and daily activities, including housing, multimodal transportation, commerce, and socialization. As the largest public spaces in cities, streets reflect the economic and social vibrancy of communities.

Great Streets are not just about streets; they are also about people. Streets are where people want to be, where a person feels comfortable and safe. Streets present interesting things to see, do, and discover. Streets have their own particular character and spirit, much like the people using the streets. People embrace this spirit and character of the streets and make it their own. Great Streets are economic drivers, offering a place where commerce can take place. Every element of Great Streets reinforces a sense of place. People go to Great Streets because they want to be part of that vibrant sense of place.

The ULI report goes on to note that by definition, Great Streets fulfill four basic responsibilities:

- They convey the quality, character, and aspirations of a neighborhood.

- They attract, stimulate, and sustain desirable economic and social activity involving any and all members of the community.

- They balance a diversity of transportation options without compromise to any mode.

- They secure and sustain stewardship by those who operate on and around the street.

What wonderful lessons there are to be learned by New Orleans stakeholders by embracing the work done in just these three recent ULI advisory panel reports. All three reports address cities and/or neighborhoods that are predominantly African American, just like New Orleans. Each city was governed by a minority chief executive at the time of the ULI panel visit—African American in both Camden and Washington, D.C., and Latino in San Antonio.

John McIlwain who chaired the Camden panel was a ULI Senior Fellow resource to the New Orleans panel. Bill Gilchrist served with John and me on the Camden panel, as well as on the New Orleans panel. Michael Banner, who chaired the ULI Great Streets panel in Washington, D.C., was with me Bill and John on the Camden panel, and has been asked by New Orleans recovery czar Edward Blakely to serve on the recovery advisory committee for that city. Mary Beth Corrigan was the ULI Vice President for Advisory Services and Policy Programs for Camden, San Antonio, Washington, D.C. and New Orleans. Clearly, ULI has exhibited its concern for cities and neighborhoods governed and populated by African Americans; and has consistently put forth solid recommendations that have guided redevelopment in such locales for over half a century.

The Great Streets planning process has created an excellent framework to begin the transformation of some of the most important corridors in Washington, D.C. As the 2006 ULI report states, it is now time for implementation. With a revised framework plan, community support, and strong leadership, the goal of creating Great Streets will be well on its way to realization. These same words could very well be spoken in relationship to New Orleans—it is now time for implementation following a revised framework with community support and strong leadership, New Orleans could well be on its way to realizing a new New Orleans.

The city of New Orleans is like a stately old mansion that has fallen into disrepair. It has been hit by winds and high water. Some of the rooms in the house are in better shape than are others. Even before the storm some of the rooms in this sprawling mansion had been ignored. Before embarking on the extensive renovation needed to restore the house to its former glory, there is the need to hire an architect to draw up a blueprint. Once the owner and architect agree on a blueprint to guide the renovation, they together hire a general contractor to carry out the rebuilding plans of the owner and architect. If the owner is smart, he will retain an owner's authorized representative, or construction manager, to manage in his stead both the architect and general contractor as they work toward a schedule to restore this grand palace fast by the river. Of course, as all parties work toward the day of completion, there are disagreements, even arguments as to how best proceed on a daily and weekly basis. Finally, once the mansion has been fully restored with a newly thought use, value and beauty not present in its original state, everyone gathers for the groundbreaking ceremony and proceed to break bread together and celebrate the rebirth of a beloved structure.

On a much larger scale, this is the challenge for New Orleans in its push to restore and recreate itself. A blueprint is needed. ULI has provided such a blueprint. We know the objections to certain elements of this blueprint. We know of the politics of redevelopment and the racial politics that have conspired to alter this blueprint. With its repopulation strategy, ULI met resistance—in some instances calling for further study in parts of the city where the damage was more severe than in other parts of the city. These areas of severe damage tended to be low-lying neighborhoods largely populated by African Americans.

In presenting its recommendations on November 18, 2005, the ULI panel emphasized that in those neighborhoods that took severe damage, definitive statements regarding the pace of redevelopment could not realistically be made until further study was undertaken. In one instance, a recent survey by urban planners and students at Cornell, Columbia University and the University of Illinois and sponsored by ACORN, concluded that the predominantly African American 9th Ward neighborhoods can be brought back largely as they existed before Hurricane Katrina flooded them. This finding contradicts the common perception that the neighborhoods are so damaged that they need to be rebuilt from scratch. The only section needing to be rebuilt according to the survey lies directly next to the levee breach on the Industrial Canal, an area that covers less than one square mile in the Lower 9th Ward. The survey found that more than 80 percent of the 9th Ward structures suffered no structural damage and that the majority of those structures were built atop piers, making it easier to raise them to meet the new flood zone requirements. Researchers and structural engineers based their assessment on the inspection of about 3,000 buildings.

Yet, after interviewing hundreds of residents, the survey concluded that the 9th Ward neighborhoods are being repopulated very slowly because of the bureaucratic and financial hurdles residents face. Only about 20 percent of the residents have returned home, the survey found. According to the survey report the data gathered shows that the 9th Ward can be rebuilt and rebuilt in a cost effective way, but what is lacking are the resources to rebuild. Many people in the 9th Ward did not have flood insurance; and government rebuilding has been slow, the ACORN report concludes. In addition, a lack of schools, day-care centers, businesses, churches, public services, and high rents are keeping people away. Local planners have concluded that a host of factors should be considered before declaring an area ready to be rebuilt, such as an area's history of flooding and the cash-strapped city's ability to provide essential services.

Another area undergoing further study relates to environmental issues. The billion dollar questions facing New Orleans are which neighborhoods will get cleaned up, which will be left contaminated, and which will be targeted as new sites to dump storm debris and waste from flooded homes. As an example, weeks after Katrina struck, the Louisiana Department of Environmental Quality (LDEQ) allowed New Orleans to reopen the 200-acre Old Gentilly Landfill in New Orleans East, the swampiest part of the city, where the majority of the population is African American. Old Gentilly is an unlined landfill, so it lacks special protective measures required by sanitary landfills, such as drains, liners, and leaching collection systems. LDEQ officials insist that the old landfill, which is still operating, meets all standards, but residents and environmentalists disagree. In April 2006, the U.S. Army Corps of Engineers and the LDEQ issued permits to allow Houston-based Waste Management, Inc., the largest commercial trash company in the country, to open a new landfill in New Orleans East.

Despite barriers and red tape, a few Katrina evacuees are slowly moving back into New Orleans's damaged homes or setting up travel trailers in their yards. Homeowners are gutting their homes, treating the mold, fixing roofs and siding, and slowly putting their lives back in order. This is the individual action necessary as part of the rebuilding process as noted by the ULI in November 2005. At the same time as this individual action is taking place, one of the main questions still hanging in the air is for returning residents is: Is this place safe? In February 2006, test results from the New York-based nonprofit Natural Resources Defense Council (NRDC) in an analysis of soil and air quality after Katrina revealed dangerously high levels of diesel fuel, lead, and other contaminants in Gentilly, Bywater, Orleans Parish, and other New Orleans neighborhoods.

In August 2006, one year after Katrina struck the city, the Environmental Protection Agency (EPA) gave New Orleans and surrounding communities a clean bill of health, while pledging to monitor a handful of toxic hot spots. Now, instead of cleaning up the mess that existed before the storm, government officials are allowing dirty neighborhoods to stay dirty forever. But can government officials really be certain that all New Orleans neighborhoods are safe? Cleanup and reconstruction efforts in New Orleans have been sluggish and patchy to date, and some contend that environmental injustice may be compounded by rebuilding on poisoned ground.

The release of ULI's report in November 2005 sparked immediate reaction. While planning and redevelopment professionals understood the reasoning behind the panel's recommendations that the city defer redevelopment of properties in severely damaged neighborhoods and focus rebuilding in the safer, higher-ground areas, many of the residents most directly affected opposed any plans that did not include immediate rebuilding in their neighborhoods. Shortly after ULI made its recommendations on a repopulation strategy, the New Orleans City Council voted unanimously to reject the plan and said residents should be allowed to rebuild wherever and whenever they chose. The further study encouraged by ULI, and as reflected in the work done in the 9th Ward and New Orleans East, cite above, bear out the wisdom of ULI's approach to the thorny issue of repopulation.

The January 2006 issue of **Urban Land** magazine is titled "Build or Bury?" As to the fate of New Orleans and its neighborhoods, this question is still extremely relevant. A reasonable blueprint to follow in relation to 'Build' remains the original ULI strategic framework. Once the political realities sink in regarding repopulation, the ULI plan will remain the most relevant guide. As to ULI's take on government effectiveness and the need for an independent redevelopment agency with appropriate resources and power as well as a financial oversight agency of a cash-strapped city, time will tell whether Nagin and his recovery czar Edward Blakely decide to follow this needed path. The balance of the ULI recommendations regarding economic development and culture, city and urban planning, housing, and infrastructure, have not been questioned in any quarters. However, time is running out on New Orleans as to its ability to rebuild itself as a stronger and more vibrant city—thus the 'Bury' option is still very much with us unless timely, decisive and difficult decisions are made and the necessary resources follow.

IX

Rebirth

"Jesus answered, 'Most assuredly, I say to you,
unless one is born of water and the Spirit,
he cannot enter the kingdom of God.'"

This passage from John 3:5 in the *Spirit Filled Life Study Bible* speaks to water and entering the kingdom of God. In this passage, water may refer to physical birth. The ULI recommendations speak to restoration, reform and rebirth. For my purposes, I posit the order as rebirth, renewal and rebuilding. Consistent with the role of water in birthing and re-birthing, it is possible that New Orleans in both a metaphorical and factual sense was filled with water and now faces the opportunity to be re-born. This state of being re-born then can perhaps propel the city toward renewal and rebuilding. Mayor Ray Nagin took a lot of heat for his 'vengeful God' statement on the Martin Luther King, Jr. holiday in January 2006. At the same time, he made reference to New Orleans as "Chocolate City" taking a cue from the Funkadelics of old. Perhaps the mayor was overcome with a need to understand the depths of the calamity and sought the Old Testament God of an eye for an eye and a tooth for a tooth for clarity. Indeed, the Big Easy—a place of drinking and debauchery, all night partying, rampant criminality, and that 'devil' music—in the Old Testament sense was a good candidate for cleansing by water. The Jordan River in the form of Lake Pontchartrain rose up and as in Genesis 7:10:

> *"And it came to pass after seven days that the waters of the flood were on the earth."*

The black-on-black crime that Mayor Nagin referred to in his 'vengeful God' remarks captures the tragedy of a 'Chocolate City' such as New Orleans. Both pre-and-post Katrina New Orleans is struggling with this dilemma whose history can be traced back to tribalism in Africa to the slave quarters in the Americas to the black ghettoes of today. The most dangerous city in the nation as of the summer of 2005 really bespoke black-on-black crime for the most part in New Orleans. The cleansing came on August 29, 2005 and in the days to follow, from an Old Testament standpoint.

As we learn in Matthew in the New Testament, 'No One Knows the Day or Hour.' As in Matthew 24:38, 39:

> *"For in the days before the flood, they were eating and drinking, marrying and giving in marriage, until the day that Noah entered the ark.*

> *and did not know until the flood came and took them all away, so also will the coming of the Son of Man be."*

Following this symbolic logic further, New Orleans was consumed by water due to both a natural and man-made disaster. Innocent lives were lost. A city was virtually destroyed and brought to its knees. People were asking 'Why me, why us?' In the aftermath of Katrina and the levee breaches, there now looms the need for a physical re-birth of the city. In this rebirth process, New Orleans has been sharply divided over two competing visions for renewal and rebuilding. One vision calls for a city with a much smaller population and physical footprint. The second vision insists that everyone should be able to return to their pre-Katrina homes.

As noted by John Beckham in the January 2006 issue of **Urban Land** magazine, "Build or Bury?", the fiscal and demographic realities of the more compact city are more realistic, while the equity and moral clarity of the right of return is very compelling. New Orleans is a city seeking hope, direction and answers in the wake of devastation. Building on President George W. Bush's pledge in New Orleans' Jackson Square in his address to the nation on September 15, 2005, that "we will do what it takes….and this great city will rise again," the BNOB action plan presented by its urban planning committee suggests that New Orleans will both be rebuilt and considered anew, providing the opportunity to revive the city's heritage while also remedying its pre-Katrina inequities and inadequacies.

This action plan envisions a new New Orleans built on the city's rich historical, cultural and architectural legacy, but reborn as a 'sustainable, environmentally safe, socially equitable community with a vibrant economy.' This statement of principle is probably agreed to by most New Orleanians, the devil, if you will, is in the details. In assessing the BNOB urban planning committee report in the **Urban Land** article, Beckman states:

> "*The urban planning committee's plan for the BNOB Commission has garnered both praise (from the Louisiana Recovery Authority, conduit for much federal assistance) and controversy—the first riff, perhaps, in what could be understood metaphorically as the city's high-stakes jazz improvization. It is a mixed metaphor, for certain, but one that captures the risks and potential rewards—as well as the spirit—of this unique city. New Orleans has stepped forward with a bold plan for its future. It is now up to the U.S. Congress to ensure that 'this great city will rise again.'*"

As noted earlier, the BNOB urban planning committee's recommendation, under the leadership of its chair Joseph Canizaro, was ultimately rejected by both the Mayor and City Council. The inability of both the Mayor and City Council to take the ULI and BNOB recommendations on repopulation served to deliver the city's recovery as 'still born' rather than set it on a path of being 're-born.' The corner that has to be turned by the city in both a real and metaphorical sense is to be 're-born' before it can restore, reform, renew and rebuild. This re-birth entails a change in attitude, a willingness to listen to outsiders, to learn to trust the judgment of others who have gone through such a post-disaster recovery, and to recognize that the issue is about rebuilding the entire city, not just my house, my neighborhood—however difficult this realization may be. Indeed, this is a huge challenge, for it is easy to be consumed by personal loss and not elevate ones mind to the collective good.

X

Renewal

Once the city in all its individual and collective parts can experience the process of being re-born, then perhaps it can move to the next phase of renewal. The term 'renewal' has taken on a negative connotation with the urban renewal programs begun in the 1960s, which in many instances became known as 'Negro removal.' Examples of misguided urban renewal can be seen in cities throughout the United States.

However, beyond this negative connotation, the transitive verb 'renew' carries all those meanings so relevant to the current state of the city of New Orleans. Renew means to begin again, make new, revive, restore to former state. Renewal as a noun refers to revival, restoration, regeneration. However, perhaps the important key word for New Orleans in its current state is 'renewability.' This is the quality of being renewable.

It is perhaps critical that the city and its citizens become re-born before the quality of being renewable exhibits itself. The manner in which the Mayor and City Council have dealt with the repopulation issue and their approach to recovery suggests the need for a change in attitude. There is considerable doubt in several quarters that 'renewability' is a noun that can be applied to the city.

An important element in this renewal process is healing. The city of New Orleans needs healing, it needs hands to be laid on it as it moves from rebirth to renewal to rebuilding. In evangelist R. W. Schambach's *The Power Book: Power Promises for Victorious Living*, in the chapter 'Power—When you need healing, Rev. Schambach includes a passage from James 5:14, 15 that has relevance for a 'sick' city:

> *"Is any sick among you? Let him call for the elders of the church; and let them pray over him, anointing him with oil in the name of the Lord: And the prayer of faith shall save the sick, and the Lord shall raise him up; and if he have committed sins, they shall be forgiven him."*

The act of renewal and change, whether in relationship to an individual or a large-scale formal organization, such as a city like New Orleans, suggests a process of being reinvigorated. There may be a variety of reasons that prompt such renewal and change to occur, but from a system standpoint it is a rational occurrence. From a rational standpoint, we expect that hurricane season will bring a number of storms into the Gulf Coast each year, for example. As rational human beings, we prepare both individually and collectively for hurricane season in a general sense and in relationship to specific storms. New Orleans and hurricanes have a long and enduring relationship to each other.

New Orleans as a large-scale formal organization is now experiencing 'problems in organizational renewal.' Again turning to classical sociological thinking on the role of organizations, Christopher Sower and Paul A. Miller (1964) state:

> *"In turning to an interpretation of the role of organizations in affecting decision making, it is necessary to start with the unique character of any formal organization. As distinguished from a community, family, or other types of social organization units, a formal organization is a social system with specific and limited goals....most organizations dealing with public issues envisage the provision of some service or goods for other persons or groups."*

As stated by sociologist Talcott Parsons (1956):

> *"An organization is a system which, as the attainment of its goal, 'produces' an identifiable something, which can be utilized in some way by another system; that is, the output of an organization is, for some other system, an input."*

This general model indicates three anchor points of legitimization for an organization: (1) the systems from which it receives its inputs of resources; (2) the values, structure, and norms which compose the organization as a system; and (3) those systems which use the output of the organization as an input. Though large-scale organizations present certain complications for society as well as for their position incumbents, they are unique social inventions. They appear to be the only social structures capable of achieving the vast and complex goals of modern society.

Yet, the problem for any society is that of planning its organizations so that desired goals are achieved, while minimizing the detrimental consequences of their functions to either the total society, or to organizational personnel. In the case of New Orleans and Hurricane Katrina, particular large-scale, formal organizations such as the city, FEMA, the White House, the State House, etc., have had their legitimacy questioned in the wake of both dealing with the storm and its aftermath and in the rebuilding of the city. Even now, local and state government are working to have a 10 percent local match in order to receive federal funds waived in the instance of New Orleans and other Gulf Coast municipalities who have seen their tax base wiped out. Such a waiver had been granted for other disasters such as Hurricane Andrew in Florida in 1992 and the September 11, 2001 terrorist attack in New York City. By granting such a waiver local officials feel the recovery can move ahead by leaps and bounds.

In this regard, economist Mancur Olson in his classic volume *The Logic of Collective Action: Public Goods and the Theory of Groups* (1965), reminds us:

> *"In other words, even if all of the individuals in a large group are rational and self-interested, and would gain if, as a group, they acted to achieve their common interest or objective, they will still not voluntarily act to achieve that common or group interest....If the members of a large group rationally seek to maximize their personal welfare, they will not act to advance their common or group objectives unless there is coercion to force them to do so....In the sharing of the costs of efforts to achieve a common goal in small groups, there is however a surprising tendency for the 'exploitation' of the great by the small."*

It can be argued in the case of the attempt by local officials in New Orleans to forge a compromise plan to guide the rebuilding process that there has been an 'exploitation of the great by the small.' Perhaps Mayor Nagin was too focused on his personal objective of being re-elected that he shied away from making tough decisions as to a repopulation strategy so as to not alienate potential voters. In the same vein, perhaps City Councilwoman Cynthia Ward-Lewis was too obsessed with her New Orleans East and 9th Ward constituency and her political survival to seek the common good of the city as a whole. Thus, the right of return which on its face seems to express a common good, and the tactic of no moratorium on rebuilding despite the severity of the damage, perhaps only prolonged the pain of the 'great' based upon decisions made by the 'small.' This pain is still evident and very visible throughout the city and wherever Katrina evacuees are spread throughout the American diaspora.

As a large-scale formal organization headed by position incumbents referred to as a mayor and city council, what are the systems from which it receives its input and resources? What are the values, structure, and norms that comprise the organization as a system?

What systems use the output of the city as a large-scale formal organization as input? Finally, what type of coercion will it take to force the position incumbents to place the common good above their personal welfare? These four questions are at the heart of the rebirth, renewal and rebuilding process that the city as a large scale formal organization and its position incumbents need to address along with those sources of input and output. The values, structure, and norms, which compose the organization are also a critical component of this model of organizational renewal and change.

From an input point of view, the city has been seeking to renew itself primarily with an eye toward securing resources from the federal government and the insurance industry. These sources of potential input have been asking for a plan of action that reflects the common good. The values, structure and norms of the city as an organization have revealed a nearly bankrupt system in terms of personal welfare being a value that has seemingly trumped the common good; one in which antiquated structures such as the planning and redevelopment functions cry out for a strong and independent entity that can carry out these important renewal functions. In addition, the historic values of the city's political elites and resultant system have not inspired confidence on the part of those sources of input into this city as an organizational system which are necessary for the city to be rebuilt. As to the output of the city as an organizational system and those other systems that use its output as input, the sustainability of the city is predicated upon increasing its output such that it has value for other organizational systems. Finally, the level and sources of coercion to force the 'small' to act rationally on behalf of the 'great' has not yet fully manifested itself. Crime and safety in the city is a potential source of coercion to move the position incumbents to act on this issue. The reality that the city will not in the short run, or perhaps even the long run, be a place populated by 450,000 to 500,000 people may be a source of coercion to act on the footprint issue and the resultant public service grid that can be achieved. The reality of the jack-o-lantern effect, both upon the city as an organizational system and individual homeowners, may ultimately serve a coercive function.

The problems of organization renewal and change are at the heart of the New Orleans dilemma. It will only be at the point that the city's leaders address the rebirthing issues in such a way as to allow a renewal and change process to ensue that a viable rebuilding plan of action can be formulated, agreed upon, and acted upon.

XI

Rebuilding

The physical rebuilding of New Orleans is part of a linked process that ties rebirth and renewal and change into a non-stochastic chain, which can restore the city and its infrastructure. That is, rebirth, renewal and rebuilding are dependent upon each other as chains in a link. A stochastic process in the language of social psychological decision-making trials laboratory studies implies an independent process between successive occurrences. However, in the case of the rebuilding of New Orleans, there is in my mind a dependence upon a rebirth thus leading to renewal and change then leading to a sustainable rebuilding process that yield a city that is guided by 'best practices' rather than 'worst practices.' Being smarter in the rebuilding process should be a goal of all of New Orleans's stakeholders—which in modern urban planning has become known as Smart Growth.

It will take leadership from the Mayor, City Council and private sector decision-makers to forge a team willing and able to pursue the public or common good in this rebuilding process. How do you build a team spirit that can lead to victory? One reason professional sports coaches such as Pat Riley and Phil Jackson are sought after and highly paid motivational speakers is that their message is often about leadership, teamwork, motivation, and putting the common good above individual needs. This same message is one that Mayor Nagin needs to emulate. His goal should be to build a creative and resolute rebuilding team intent on making New Orleans a victor in the smart growth conference of cities. After all, his message in his initial victory as mayor of the city was one of doing away with the politics of the past that hurt the city's credibility. He went against the norm in terms of the political culture of the city. He has needed to go against the norm in relationship to the challenge of rebuilding his crippled city.

A January 4, 2007 *Washington Post* article "New Orleans Repeats Mistakes as It Rebuilds; Many Houses Built in Areas Katrina Flooded Are Not on Raised Foundations," tells the same old story.

> *"By ones and twos, homeowners here are reinhabiting neighborhoods, even the most devastated ones, and many view their return as a triumph over adversity. But experts involved in the rebuilding believe that the helter-skelter return of residents to this low-lying metropolis may represent another potential disaster..... The chairman of the federal Gulf Coast rebuilding office, Donald E. Powell, said recently that 'tough decisions' about where to repopulate this half-empty city are necessary."*

Powell goes on to state that both he and President Bush believe planning decisions should not be made in Washington, but rather at the local level. He goes on to note that at some point there needs to be strong local leadership, and that includes making tough decisions about the city's size and the safety of its citizens.

In the December/January 2006-07 issue of *The Planning Report: The Insider's Guide to Managed Growth,* New Orleans recovery czar Edward Blakely spoke about his strategy for reviving New Orleans. In this interview, Blakely says his job is to coordinate all the city agencies and subordinate agencies to rebuild New Orleans. Blakely indicates he will be coordinating all funds, whether public or private, that come into the city for rebuilding purposes. Blakely goes on to note that most of the debris has been removed and that the city is functioning. Sewers, water and electricity are working and most of the necessary assets are back in place. He also notes that building stock has been damaged to the extent that it has to be rebuilt in most residential areas.

Blakely says he told Nagin in his job interview with the Mayor that the city needed to get out of the planning mode and get into the action mode, i.e., we have to start building some things in order to restore public confidence. He went on to state in this interview with Nagin that we have to set up a system so that people who want to come back can come back somewhere in New Orleans as soon as possible. This return to the city might be in stages and they might come back to one area of the city, and then they might move into other neighborhoods in a year or two.

Blakely goes on to state in The Planning Report interview that the old New Orleans was built for the 18th century, and that system was not functional. He sees the rebuilding as one that will follow a smart growth or New Urban platform. Further, since no one was in charge of the rebuilding everyone has been operating in a fragmented way. His goal is to organize a 'recovery consul' to bring people all under one umbrella and sort out an action plan similar to an accepted approach use to develop a master-planned community.

Blakely further states that one of the reasons FEMA has not released funds is that the city has not put a rebuilding plan in place, i.e., they need to know what they are releasing funds to. Are you restoring this building just because it is available, or is it part of some plan? That's federal law, Blakely states. The federal government is insisting that there needs to be a clear plan as to where you want to put assets. That is, why do you want to put assets in this particular location, how much funding is needed, and what is your timeframe and capability to put this asset on line.

As to the New Orleans political reputation that it is extremely difficult to find any consensus and take dramatic action, Blakely states that there are several reasons for this commonly held impression. One is that local government has not been trusted at any level. Everyone thinks they can do better and that attitude hampers any recovery effort because people decide to do their own thing and dare the government to stop them. He recognizes this aspect of the rebuilding process is going to be a big challenge, but that people have been approaching him and saying they want to be on his team and work with him in this process.

Blakely goes on to state in The Planning Report interview that most of his benchmarks for the first six months will not be very visible. First priority is to get the federal funds flowing; and that will be facilitated by having a concrete plan to spend the funds. The second priority is to mount some demonstration projects to show the kinds of settlement patterns we want so people understand where we're going. The third priority is to have a communications system so that everyone knows what we are doing. In this regard, he wants every resident to be able to call someone who can work with them to bring them back, and when people come back into the city they are going to be case-managed in the locations we want. That won't be very visible in terms of rebuilding the city, but it will set the framework.

As to The Planning Report question of:

What is New Orleans' population today, and what do you think it will be in two years?

Blakely responds:

> *"The population is around 200,000, and in two years it will go up only about 20,000 or 30,000 more. But then after that first wave of development, things will happen very fast. So five years out the city might be over 500,000."*

It was January 8, 2007 that Edward Blakely spent his first day as recovery czar for the city of New Orleans. It was almost precisely one year earlier in January 2006 that both Mayor Nagin and the City Council rejected a ULI and BNOB plan that mirrors statements made by Blakely. In essence, due to a lack of leadership the city of New Orleans has forfeited one year in its rebuilding timeline.

Blakely talks about putting together a team and lack of trust in local government. He talks about leadership and principles of smart growth. He talks about a staging strategy for repopulating the city. He also brings to the rebuilding table some innovative ideas as to how to diversify and grow the local economy, how to strengthen the public schools, as well as the role of local colleges and universities. Perhaps New Orleans has found its 'recovery coach' one who can forge a sense of teamwork among a stressed-out and over-matched rank of elected officials and private sector leaders.

In *Urban Land* magazine's February 2007 issue there is a special section which provides a Regional Spotlight: Gulf Coast. In this section it is noted that New Orleans is about to complete one of the most comprehensive planning processes—neighborhood by neighborhood—ever undertaken in America, according to President Kabacoff. He notes that a rebuilding czar with great credentials has been retained to lead the effort. Kabacoff goes on to state that it is hoped that this will provide the city with good leadership, which will allow the city to move forward.

EDSA, a Ft. Lauderdale, Florida-based planning, landscape architecture, urban design, and graphic design firm conducted assessment and planning services for three districts under the Unified New Orleans Plan (UNOP)—these being Lakeview, Algiers, and New Orleans East, Village de l'Est and Venetian Isles—which are being treated as one district. Proposed plans for Lakeview include developing high-rise condominiums and turning a high school into a seniors' housing; creating a community development corporation to redevelop vacant residential property; and offering incentives for small businesses to return to two corridors in the neighborhood.

Plans for New Orleans East range from attracting commercial investment to arteries with infrastructure improvements and reopening police and fire stations, schools, community health centers, to limiting expansion of multifamily housing. In addition, the state of Louisiana has been encouraged to utilize a portion of the $10 billion in Community Development Block Grant (CDBG) funds with the Low Income Tax Credit (LIHTC) program, which was increased by a factor of ten for three years via the federally financed Gulf Opportunity Zone (GO Zone) incentives to spur mixed-income projects.

The work that EDSA, and others, are doing in New Orleans is a direct spinoff from ULI's strategies for rebuilding. When ULI issued its strategies to the Bring New Orleans Back Commission on November 18, 2005, it asserted that its work was not the end, but merely the beginning. Included in the current discussion as to repopulating the city is the notion of 'clustering' so as to achieve more efficiencies in the delivery of city services. One of the dilemmas in any repopulation strategy has been achieving an appropriate match between a beleaguered city providing essential services over a footprint that needs to constrict in the short run, and perhaps expand out again in the long run if rebuilding reality merited such a strategy.

But as Tom Murphy reminds us in this same February 2007 issue of *Urban Land* magazine,

> *"Hurricane Katrina has created a leadership laboratory. For any building in New Orleans to come out of the ground, someone has had to will it to happen. What has been seen is numbing bureaucracies more focused on process than results, a population battered and suspicious, and nearly everyone focused on today—leaving little energy to think about tomorrow.*
>
> *All this must be overcome in order for the needed building to take place."*

My wish as an interested and involved outsider is that Ed Blakely can be such a leader—the Red Auerbach or Phil Jackson for New Orleans—a tough talking taskmaster who can get his distracted and nettlesome team to act in concert with one clear goal in mind—Victory for the City of New Orleans—and for the nation as a whole!

XII

A New New Orleans

When I arrived in New Orleans on November 12, 2005 for the ULI Expert Team and Advisory Panel meetings, one of the first people I saw when I arrived at the Sheraton New Orleans Hotel on Canal Street was ULI Senior Fellow for Housing John McIlwain. He was proudly sporting a slick black t-shirt that said 'ReNew Orleans' on the front. I am a t-shirt guy, so I asked John where he got it and if I could get one too. John said he had purchased it at a shop in Georgetown not too far from ULI's headquarters in Washington, D.C. I pleaded with him to buy one for me and send it to me in Los Angeles. That t-shirt perfectly captured the task ahead, not only for ULI, but also for the city of New Orleans, the state of Louisiana, and the nation.

Once I arrived back in Los Angeles, I received a package from John. It included that wonderful t-shirt as well as a note. In the note John reminded me that at our preparation meeting on the night of Thursday, November 17, 2005 as we went over our presentation for the following morning and we were agonizing over how to best present our strategy for repopulation, we knew our recommendation would be controversial. Joe Brown wondered aloud whether we would be run out of town. In John's note, he reminded me that I had stated, "Sometimes it's okay to be run out of town."

Indeed, our repopulation recommendation was not only controversial, but it was fully misunderstood. This particular recommendation was run out of town only to return in the form of New Orleans's recovery czar over one year later. Clearly, Blakely stated strategy of a staged repopulation of the neighborhoods is another way of saying there will be a sequential investment strategy that will be predicated upon having a coherent plan that can guide the federal funds in a still difficult rebuilding process.

Having lost more than a year in developing a plan of action, it is particularly ironic that Blakely, in January 2007, stated that the city needs to stop planning and start some action. Since we have doubled back on the process of planning for the rebuilding of the new New Orleans, let's revisit the action plan that could have been in place in January 2006, such that by January 2007 when Blakely came on the scene there could have been nearly one year of action under way.

John Beckman's 'A New Action Plan for New Orleans' in **Urban Land** magazine's January 2006 issue "Build or Bury?" identifies three types of rebuilding opportunities:

- Immediate opportunity areas are those located on high ground or requiring demolition and clearance, where large, relatively vacant sites can be planned and developed in the near term.

- Infill development areas are those located on high ground or requiring demolition and clearance, where large, relatively vacant sites can be planned and developed in the near term.

- Neighborhood planning areas are those where, because of heavy flooding and damage, a more detailed planning and outreach process needs to be undertaken before redevelopment.

Within these three areas, the action plan also targets five areas with short-term potential for construction of significant numbers of new houses, the lack of which is the biggest constraint to repopulation.

The ULI Advisory Panel articulated three principles for framing rebuilding decisions for rebuilding New Orleans:

- Plans should be faithful to what makes New Orleans unique— its rich culture, history, and 'old urbanist' neighborhood design.

- Natural and engineered solutions must be balanced to meet infrastructure needs. As New Orleans designs and strengthens its flood protection, its engineered system—levees, seawalls, drainage canals, and pumping stations—can be supplemented by restoring natural areas within the city and building in concert with its topography.

- Recovery must be equitable, sustainable, and mobilize as many citizens as possible. The reconstruction process can begin in those areas that are safe and offer immediate opportunities for restoration and development. Severely damaged areas of the city will require more detailed evaluation and community input for decisions regarding restoration, and these decisions must be made through a transparent and fair process.

ULI Advisory Panel member Patrick Phillips chaired the Economic Development and Culture sub-group while in New Orleans. In the January 2006 issue of **Urban Land**, in 'Thoughts on New Orleans,' Patrick states that this team organized its findings and recommendations around three perspectives.

> *"First is the near-term rebuilding effort, which is in its early stages and which will be the dominant job creator in New Orleans for perhaps the next five years....Equally important is to get those sectors of the economy that were relatively strong—tourism, the universities, health care, and the port—back on their feet as soon as possible.... And in the third perspective, over the long run New Orleans has an opportunity to restructure its economy on a more diverse and sustainable platform. This new economy will require, more than any other factor, a clear strategic vision and a new, sector-based approach to economic development."*

Local real estate developer Pres Kabacoff in **Urban Land's** January 2006 issue on "Bury or Build?" says he expects New Orleans will eventually be a denser city along the high ground. Kabacoff feels the city is going to lose population across the board, from young professionals who can relocate elsewhere, to the poor who cannot return or have nothing to return to. Kabacoff further states:

> *"I do not see an exclusive group coming back. If we have 250,000 people, we will be fortunate."*

ULI Advisory Panel member Warren Whitlock in his January 2006 **Urban Land** magazine article titled "Rebuilding the Soul of New Orleans" states that New Orleans will be reborn. The issue is how the city will be rebuilt—and how long it will take to revitalize areas critical to its economic sustainability. The New Orleans levees are but one of the infrastructure systems that need to be rebuilt safely and swiftly, Whitlock continues. Ongoing debate about appropriate levee protection centers on whether to rebuild the levees to the pre-Katrina level intended to protect the city from a Category 3 hurricane, or to build a vastly more complicated and expensive system capable of withstanding Category 5 storms.

Charles Picciola in this same "Bury or Build?" issue of **Urban Land** in his article titled 'Louisiana's Coastal Plight" argues that for the present and the future, it is critical that the area be rebuilt with an adequate buffer in place between the city and the Gulf of Mexico. Picciola further states that should the long overdue coastal wetlands problem not be adequately addressed, there will be little reason to rebuild the city. The reality is that south Louisiana is gradually sinking into the Gulf of Mexico at the rate of 25 to 35 square miles per year—and events such as Katrina only serve to accelerate this process. Since 1930, some 1,900 square miles of coastal wetlands, the size of the state of Delaware, have been lost to the Gulf of Mexico.

Picciola goes on to remind us that the major cause of Katrina's extreme devastation to the city of New Orleans is that the wetlands act as a speed bump for storm surges caused by hurricanes. If the current state of wetlands erosion continues, New Orleans will be left increasingly vulnerable to the potential storm surge brought by every approaching hurricane season.

Experts familiar with the problem estimate that it will cost $14 billion and take nearly 20 years to reverse these effects, says Picciola. He concludes his discussion of Louisiana's coastal plight by stating unequivocally:

> *"Without the rebuilding of Louisiana's wetlands, the future of New Orleans is jeopardized."*

Clearly, as articulated in the ULI Expert Team and Advisory Panel's strategic thinking, one important goal is to make the water a friend to the city of New Orleans rather than an enemy. This objective is reasonable considering the city's geography. The city is nestled precariously among the Mississippi River, Lake Pontchartrain, and vast swampland, which is the reason it is often called the Isle of Orleans. Adding to the city's vulnerability is the fact that the major portion of the city lies below sea level.

Given this geographic reality, how can the surrounding water be made a friend rather than an enemy? One answer to this daunting question is rooted in the role parks and open space will play in a rebuilt New Orleans. In the October 2006 issue of *Urban Land*, Jennifer Hall's article "Visions of Green" she describes several attempts by the design community to craft a vision for the city's future. One example is a proposal by Cambridge, Massachusetts-based Hargreaves Associates in which they envision fixing the infrastructure and making it a park. Hargreaves Associates also argues for protection through-out the city from a category 5 hurricane to include large levees also serving as public open spaces and crossed by a network of bridges. Assuming everyone is not exercising the right of return, this vision argues that with the remnant lots you could then broker your way to connect these lots, creating cross-town connections. These inter-connected greenways could have many uses, including serving as localized stormwater management, urban wildlife habitats, and pedestrian and bike trails.

Mary Vogel's article "Moving Toward High-Performance Infra-structure" in this same **Urban Land** issue points out how Portland, Oregon and Seattle, Washington are leading the way in redefining their streets to be a critical part of the public realm rather than just thoroughfares for cars, and in using the land to help manage storm-water runoff. Given New Orleans recovery czar Edward Blakely's focus on building a modern city and his realization that in so doing the city will have to re-do a lot of streets, the Portland and Seattle cases can be instructive. Portland and Seattle have perhaps come closest to designing natural stormwater management for an urban density that is perhaps replicable in New Orleans. Portland's 12th Avenue is a model for fitting nature-based stormwater manage-ment into the traditional street network in moderate-to-high density areas, notes Vogel. She further states that Seattle's 'Swale on Yale' and Taylor 28 move further in the direction of high perfor-mance infrastructure.

In the January 2006 issue of **Urban Land,** Mark Muro and Bruce Katz in "Raising the Roof in New Orleans" delineate what they describe as the proper outline for reconstruction including:

- Greater New Orleans's unbalanced, unsafe development pat-terns must be bent toward safer, more sustainable development.

- A largely segregated neighborhood map must be replaced with a far more mixed, inclusive pattern, one characterized by what can be called 'neighborhoods of choice and connection.'

- Plan where to rebuild—systematically and democratically.

- Rebuild crucial infrastructure.

- Use reconstruction money to promote sound land use and high quality city design.

- Restore the Delta.

In this same issue of **Urban Land**, Kevin Shanley in "Rebuilding the Gulf Coast" states:

- First, we must determine where new development is safe from storm damage and therefore remains inappropriate.

- Second, we must use the latest storm surge and flood-control technologies to safeguard major coastline and river communities from flooding.

- Third, we must avoid using outdated flood control measures that only exacerbate problems.

- Fourth, we must make greater use of natural flood management systems—wetlands, rivers, bayous, and floodplains—to handle stormwater more effectively.

- Fifth, we must bite the bullet and redevelop low-lying flood--prone sites—where residents and businesses will always face risk from future storms—as natural sites that become community amenities and detain stormwater.

- Finally, all new development must actually reduce stormwater peak flows and improve runoff water quality.

Tom Murphy in *Urban Land* (January 2006) in "A Call for Action in New Orleans" states that we desperately need translators in order to create a new New Orleans. Translators are those who can communicate across the divisions, get us unstuck from the processes we put ourselves in to protect from each other. Murphy argues we need translators all across America, but no more importantly than in New Orleans where we need decisions to be made quickly, accurately and in a humane fashion.

As noted earlier, I first met New Orleans's recovery czar Edward Blakely when I was project manager for the West Angeles Cathedral in South Los Angeles beginning over ten years ago. He showed up at my construction office on Crenshaw Boulevard one day in 1998 to look at the plans for this 5,000-seat sanctuary. Just as I needed God to help me build this massive cathedral, so too does Blakely need to pray each and every day as he endeavors to create the new New Orleans. He is correct when he states that the time for planning is past, and now we need some action. But he also needs a higher power by his side.

This reaching out to God is reflected in a January 4, 2007 *Washington Post* article:

> *"Rochelle Krantz, 64, and her husband are repairing their home in Chalmette....Sometimes complete strangers, she said, come up to ask: 'You're coming back?' And then they say, 'You're nuts!'....'We'll leave it in the good Lord's hands,' Krantz said....'It's terrifying: We're doing the same things we have in the past but expecting different results,' said Robert Bea, a professor of civil engineering at the University of California at Berkeley and a former New Orleans resident who served as a member of the National Science Foundation panel that studied the city's levees.... 'People always say, 'I'm going to pray,' said Bea, the Berkeley civil engineer, 'And I'm thinking, 'I hope God is listening.'"*

Perhaps the scripture I had in a frame in the West Angeles Cathedral construction office is also appropriate for Ed Blakely and Mayor Nagin as they endeavor to rebuild New Orleans. Nehemiah 2:20 says:

> *"So I answered them, and said to them, 'The God of Heaven Himself will prosper us; therefore we His servants will arise and build...'*

New Orleans will arise and build—and in so doing it shall prosper. The least of thee shall come to the fore. These are spiritual times in New Orleans and mere hexes will not do. It is going to take teamwork, motivation, leadership and a whole lot of praying in order to ReNew Orleans.

Conclusion

This concluding chapter contains three of my articles that are reprinted from **Urban Land** magazine that can serve as best practice case studies in the redevelopment process now underway in New Orleans.

The first of these articles is "Hollywood's Time to Shine" from the September 2005 issue of the magazine. In this article I describe the revitalization of Hollywood, California, perhaps the most famous neighborhood in the world. This is my neighborhood of 250,000 people within a city of 3.7 million. I have everything I need here in Hollywood. Like New Orleans, Hollywood is a brand name known the world over. Like Hollywood, New Orleans can use this brand identity as part of its revitalization strategy. Not too long ago, Hollywood was a neighborhood considered to be seedy and dangerous. Today, Hollywood is lively and vital, hosting nearly 10 million tourists annually. Hollywood, like much of Los Angeles also had to recover from two recent disasters. One of these disasters, the 1994 Northridge earthquake, was a natural disaster that did billions of dollars of damage. The second disaster, the urban riots of 1992, tore up the physical and psychological fabric of the city—again doing hundreds of millions of dollars of property damage. Hollywood has recovered nicely from both these disasters—and can offer a beacon of hope for the city of New Orleans.

Hollywood's Time to Shine

Philip S. Hart and Maureen McAvey

Once the epicenter of the entertainment industry, Hollywood is finding new life, new residents, and new business thanks to ambitious redevelopment plans.

Hollywood, California, is one of the most famous and recognizable communities in the world. It is also a historic district, primarily associated with the movie industry. From the early days of the film industry up until the late 1960s and early 1970s, Hollywood remained at the center of the film, television, and music industries.

Around the mid-1970s and on into the 1980s, the area fell on hard times, with much of the entertainment activity that had been centered in Hollywood moving further west and north, leaving behind a few vestiges—Capitol Records, Paramount Studios, and Sunset Gower Studios. During this time, Hollywood gradually declined, gaining the reputation of being crime ridden and seedy. Despite this reversal of fortune, the

neighborhood continued to be a key destination for tourists from around the world, and remains so to this day. During the mid- to late 1970s, it was increasingly recognized that a concerted effort would have to take place to revive this moribund community.

The city of Los Angeles's Community Redevelopment Agency (CRA), along with local organizations such as the Hollywood Group—urban planners and architects located in the Pantages Theater offices on Hollywood Boulevard—and the Hollywood Chamber of Commerce, began focusing on revitalization strategies for the area. On May 7, 1986, the Hollywood Redevelopment Plan was adopted by a Los Angeles city council ordinance. The plan specified the project area boundary and legal description, redevelopment plan goals, and proposed redevelopment activities. The Hollywood Redevelopment Project area (as drawn by the CRA) encompasses 1,107 acres in the heart of Hollywood.

Along with Hollywood's longtime booster and honorary "mayor" Johnny Grant, city councilwoman Jackie Goldberg was a strong advocate for revitalization of the neighborhood. The late John Ferraro, in his role as city council president, also worked hard to direct resources to his Hollywood district. The residential communities around Hollywood, such as Hollywood Hills, Hancock Park and Los Feliz, remained strong bastions of middle-class and upper-middle-class residents. The city council successors to both Goldberg and Ferraro—Eric Garcetti and Tom LaBonge—took the Hollywood baton effectively and helped move revitalization plans ahead.

Today, after years of starts and stops (including the 1992 riots), a number of major redevelopment projects are either completed or underway. More than $2 billion of commercial and residential development within the boundaries of this historic Los Angeles neighborhood either has been completed or is on the drawing board. This mix of developments includes over 2 million square feet of space encompassing mixed-use commercial and residential, historic rehabilitation, entertainment company, and other sector expansion and relocation, as well as public improvements. There are three Red Line subway stops in Hollywood connecting the community to the San Fernando Valley and downtown L.A., and tourists continue to arrive by the millions each year.

In March 2001, an Urban Land Institute (ULI) advisory services panel visited and looked at market potential, planning and design issues, development strategies, and implementation plans for Hollywood. The report published after this visit, titled "A Strategy for Hollywood's Comeback," is helping guide the revitalization efforts now underway. Since the time of the visit, the 9/11 terrorist attacks threw the local and national economies into a tailspin, affecting Hollywood as well. On a positive note, in March 2002 the new Kodak Theatre in the Hollywood and Highland complex became home to the Academy Awards, returning the venerable event, once hosted at Hollywood's Roosevelt Hotel, to the neighborhood most closely associated with the movie industry.

Although Hollywood was incorporated as an independent city in 1903, it was annexed by the city of Los Angeles in 1910. A secession referendum seeking to restore Hollywood's independence appeared on the ballot on November 5, 2002, but was voted down. On May 17, 2005, a new Los Angeles mayor, Antonio Villaraigosa, was elected, defeating incumbent James Hahn.

Mayor Villaraigosa, who took office on July 1, has clearly signaled the importance of Hollywood to the city of L.A.—one of his first visits as mayor-elect was to Hollywood, taking a stroll down Hollywood Boulevard with Hollywood's "Mayor" Grant to deliver a speech on "runaway production," or how to keep TV and film production in Hollywood, at the historic Roosevelt Hotel.

Since the March 2001 ULI panel visit, several fairly significant events have taken place in Hollywood, greater Los Angeles, the nation, and the world. These transforming events seemingly did not alter Hollywood's march toward renewal. The Hollywood Economic Development Update 2005, titled "The Status of Development in Hollywood," released by the Hollywood Chamber of Commerce at its June 17, 2005, annual economic summit, captures this vitality. The report briefly describes 19 new commercial/retail projects; 16 new nightclubs/restaurants; three new or renovated hotels; 21 new residential/mixed-use projects; six office rehabilitations/new tenants; two medical facilities; and four educational facilities.

The Hollywood and Vine project, to be developed by Legacy Partners of Foster City, California, and Gatehouse Capital of Dallas, is the largest project currently in development in Hollywood. The proposed project would occupy 4.56 acres. A $325 million project is planned, which will include a 296-room W Hotel (managed by Starwood Hotels and Resorts Worldwide), 350 apartment units (20 percent of which are slated to be affordable housing), 145 luxury condominiums, approximately 60,000 square feet of ground-level retail space, an international transit plaza, and 1,219 spaces of below-grade parking. Ground breaking is expected to take place in mid-2006, with occupancy beginning in 2008.

Adjacent to the Hollywood and Vine project is the proposed Nederlander site and its estimated $300 million mixed-use entertainment-themed development. Under a 99-year ground lease of this seven-acre site, the New York City—based Clarett Group plans to build a large-scale, mixed-use project featuring up to 1,000 residential units on land adjacent to the Pantages Theatre. The project is planned to be built in phases following a 12- to 14-month entitlement period. To the maximal degree possible, it is important for area planning purposes that the developers of these two large-scale projects just across the street from each other engage in a collaborative planning and design process so that appropriate integration can be achieved in the built environment at Hollywood and Vine.

The project at Hollywood and Highland can be instructive as to how to proceed with the proper execution of these two large projects. Hollywood and Highland, a $615 million mixed-use project developed by Trizec Properties, Inc. of Chicago (formerly TrizecHahn), was hurt by the impact of 9/11 on tourism. The retail uses at the project had been geared more to the tourist market than to the local market, so between the

time of the attacks and the November 2001 opening of Holly-wood and Highland, the priority market for its retail offerings had dried up. The mall itself has design problems, beginning with the vertical nature of the retail space and its confusing layout. Further, the parking rates at opening were much higher than L.A.-area retail customers were used to paying, despite the ULI panelists' recommendation in March 2001 that accessible and affordable parking would best serve the development; the rates have since been lowered. By spring 2004, Trizec had sold Hollywood and Highland to the CIM Group for a mere $201 million, which was not good for Trizec, but was good for Hollywood.

Despite its flaws, the development at Hollywood and High-land represents a significant investment at this location, and helped stimulate other interest and activity—tourists are coming back to Hollywood in droves, the Oscars are seen by a billion people worldwide each year from the Kodak Theatre, and the CIM Group is a local owner/developer/financier that can make Hollywood and Highland work. The relatively strong restaurant, movie theater, entertainment, and hotel components in this development can only grow stronger once the retail segment strengthens.

These days, real estate professionals are expressing their optimism for Hollywood and the neighboring West Hollywood and mid-Wilshire area. Increasingly popular among investors, mixed-use developments are becoming more attractive in high-density areas such as the Hollywood market. Residential units within a mixed-use context also are becoming a trend in Hollywood, as evinced by the recently completed Sunset and Vine project. In 2004, the Bond Companies of Santa Monica and Canyon Johnson Realty Advisors of Beverly Hills completed this mixed-use project with 300 apartments in 2004 for $120 million and sold it in 2005 to SSR Realty Advisors—now Black Rock Realty Group, based in Morristown, New Jersey—for close to $165 million.

Smaller residential projects are also moving forward in Hollywood. Hollywood Hillview, LLC, is rehabilitating a historic building on Hollywood Boulevard to restore its 54 residential units. In addition, there will be 2,000 square feet of retail space on the ground floor and 10,000 square feet of commercial space in the basement. The Cosmo Street Lofts, an adaptive use project being developed by Creative Environments of Hollywood, consists of an existing four-story, 40,000-square-foot warehouse being converted into 47 live/work lofts. The Broadway Building at the corner of Hollywood and Vine is another adaptive use project now under construction by the KOR Group of Los Angeles. This former department store will be converted into 96 condominiums with 152 on-site parking spaces along with ground-floor retail. At the corner of Sunset and Vine, the CIM Group is planning an adaptive use project in the Sunset Vine Tower that will feature 90 residential units and 15,000 square feet of retail space.

These residential developments reflect the ULI panel's view that demand exists for 500 to 1,000 multifamily housing units at various price points. If the residential developments that either have been completed or are in the pipeline reach the market, then this demand, it is hoped, will have been more than met. The ULI panel also suggested that Hollywood plan for a new upscale boutique hotel. While some of the multi-family housing demand will be met by residential units at the Hollywood and Vine mixed-use project, the project includes a W Hotel, too. The panel also recommended that existing hotels be rehabilitated. Indeed, a $25 million renovation of the Roosevelt Hotel is nearing completion. Given its rich cinematic history, this 248-room hotel, which opened in 1927, may be poised to become a destination for the Hollywood glitterati.

With its three aforementioned Red Line subway stations, Hollywood is uniquely positioned to take advantage of transit-oriented development (TOD). The tools that aid in the implementation of TOD include the following: a market-based site and phasing plan;

land assembly; infrastructure investment; shared parking; expedited permits and reviews; and direct financial participation. The Hollywood and Highland station was the first out of the box, which with about 117,000 boardings every weekday is the busiest Metropolitan Transit Authority (MTA) line. This project scored fairly high in its execution on each of these six TOD criteria. Design flaws and external events have affected the success of this mixed-use project, but it remains a viable example of TOD within an urban context. Hollywood and Western is the second station where TOD is taking place. Either completed or in the pipeline is a mix of retail, residential (both market rate and affordable), and parking. Finally, at Hollywood and Vine, right across Hollywood Boulevard from the Nederlander's Pantages Theatre mentioned earlier, is a $325 million mixed-use project that grades high on these six TOD criteria. Taken together, these three Hollywood Red Line stations are an example of well-thought-out TOD in this historic neighborhood.

Even with the recent TOD successes in Hollywood, the challenge of leveraging the power of mass transit remains. As the ULI panel report notes, the subway system is a powerful resource for the community. Hollywood can advance its revitalization efforts through TOD and public transportation incentives. Few communities in the United States have three subway stations at their front door. The existing subway and light-rail systems, which connect to an extensive bus network, provide Hollywood with regional access superior to that of any other community in the Los Angeles basin. Finally, the challenge of leveraging the power of mass transit ties into the increasing traffic congestion in Hollywood that is attendant to its redevelopment success. As traffic congestion worsens, the Metro Rail will become even more of an asset. If the Metro Rail is marketed appropriately, it has the potential to become a major tourist convenience, serving many who wish to visit multiple sites over a period of several days without the burden of renting a car or riding a tour bus.

On the medical front, between Children's Hospital and Kaiser Permanente Hospital, over $800 million of construction either has been completed or is in the pipeline. (See "Community Hospitals," page X.) Both of these medical facilities are looking to 2007 as the completion date for their ambitious expansion plans in their east Hollywood locations. This construction activity will bring both hospitals up to current seismic codes, as well as add a combined total of 735 beds.

The success of the redevelopment of Hollywood is partly attributable to the two strong business improvement district (BID) organizations there. Launched in December 1996, the Hollywood Entertainment District BID is a property-based BID spanning an 18-block stretch of Hollywood Boulevard and 180 property owners. The purpose of the BID is to attract entertainment-related businesses back to Hollywood. The second successful BID in Hollywood is the Hollywood Media District, a benefit assessment district that represents more than 200 property owners. The success of these two BIDs has led to the development of two other BIDS, one in east Hollywood and the other on Sunset Boulevard. Though not yet operational, it is anticipated that both BIDs will be up and running in the near future.

Hollywood nightlife is red-hot. Nightclubs and restaurants are hopping up and down Hollywood and Sunset Boulevards, as well as on Cahuenga Boulevard and Vine Street. People young and old are in the street and on the sidewalks, sometimes club-hopping on foot, defying the myth the Angelenos always drive from place to place. Today's young stars populate these Hollywood venues, sometimes as investors. The trick in the Hollywood nightclub business is to continually reinvent yourself: although you may be hot today, you could be left out in the cold tomorrow as the action moves on, usually to another spot in Hollywood.

What is next for Hollywood? Having seemingly reinvented itself, this historic neighborhood is now viewed as a desirable place to do business, to live, to party, to eat out, to be entertained, to worship, and to shop. It is no longer regarded as seedy and dangerous, though crime, drug use, and homelessness remain issues of concern. Indeed, Hollywood is renewing itself to the extent that local stakeholders have positioned the community to possibly be the site of the Academy of Motion Pictures' proposed 200,000-square-foot museum.

By all appearances, Hollywood has turned the corner and is on the way back up. Much has been accomplished, but much more remains to be done. Indeed, it is now Hollywood's time to shine.

Philip S. Hart is president/CEO of Hart Realty Advisors, a division of Tanya Hart Communications, Inc., in Hollywood. Along with the American City Coalition, Hart cosponsored the March 2001 ULI advisory services panel visit to Hollywood. Maureen McAvey is senior resident fellow of urban development at the Urban Land Institute.

24-Hour Shine @Poet-broker

Developers are tinkering with a tinsel town toolkit
chiseling clues from foundations of urban places,
they've tightened up synergy in boulevard spaces,
and smoothed diverse urban energies into grooves.
The past is preserved in Egyptian and Pantages Restorations
the future is foreshadowed on the rails of three transit stations
at night workers race to bars over walk of fame pavement
then throw off their shoes in lofts above the rail tubes.
The barely lit sun shines on reborn deco buildings
where youth rests before stumbling past steamy cafés
up to loft offices or down Hollywood and Vine escalators
to catch red neon Metro to Downtown or San Fernando gigs,
looking back above them at glass towers where elevators
mix women in nurses whites with sisters in St. John knits.

Ed Rosenthal is a "poet-broker" in Los Angeles and is also a historic properties specialist for CB Richard Ellis, where he is senior vice president of investments.

Reprinted with permission of ULI-Urban Land Institute, Washington, DC.

The second article is titled "Boston's Parcel to Parcel Linkage Plan: Guiding Downtown Prosperity to the Needy Neighborhoods." This article from the July 2005 issue of **Urban Land** describes an innovative parcel-to-parcel linkage plan that economically connects a parcel of land in Boston's booming downtown with a parcel of land in the needy Roxbury neighborhood. On page 34 of the ULI report **New Orleans, Louisiana: A Strategy for Rebuilding** in the section on economic development and culture in discussing the film and television industry it is recommended that:

> *"One possible development strategy for this sector is to economically connect either the west bank studio facility or the CBD studio facility with the teaching studio in the Ninth Ward. This type of parcel-to-parcel linkage strategy has proven successful for projects such as the 36-story One Lincoln office tower in downtown Boston and the nine-story office building at Renaissance Park in Boston's needy Roxbury neighborhood."*

Boston's Parcel-to-Parcel Linkage Plan

Philip S. Hart

An innovative linkage plan is helping guide downtown prosperity to Boston's needy neighborhoods.

The story of Boston's parcel-to-parcel linkage plan began more than 50 years ago. To make downtown Boston more accessible to commuters from the city's growing and distant suburbs, a system of highways, which included the Southwest Expressway and the Inner Belt, was first proposed in 1948. Land was cleared for the right-of-way for the Southwest Expressway in 1966. In response to pressure from a wide range of groups operating under the slogan of "People Before Highways," the state's then-governor, Francis W. Sargent, declared a moratorium on construction in 1970. After a study of regional transportation needs conducted by the Boston Transportation Planning Review (BTPR), Sargent

Peter Vanderwalder/Jung Brannen Associates, Inc.

decided against the proposed highway construction, although the relocation of the Orange Line rapid transit from its elevated structure to the existing Penn Central right-of-way would be executed as planned.

The decision in 1972 to veto the construction of the Southwest Expressway through several Boston neighborhoods made possible an opportunity to engage in planning to meet the needs of local residents. Roxbury was one of the neighborhoods affected. At the time it was home to a predominantly African American population. This largely low-income neighborhood suffered greatly from extensive demolition in anticipation of the proposed highway construction between 1966 and 1970. The area would become known as the Southwest Corridor— and by the early 1970s barren open spaces were the norm. Demolition within the corridor had an extreme effect on the social and economic development of the area— including disinvestment by banks and a series of fires. Nearly 200 acres of vacant land remained once the dust settled.

Attention then turned to the redevelopment of this formerly bustling urban core within a stone's throw of the thriving Back Bay neighborhood. The commonwealth of Massachusetts established the Southwest Corridor Land Development Coordinator's Office, headed up by Anthony Pangaro, to guide the planning and development process. Over 50 community organizations came together as the Southwest Corridor Land Development Coalition, Inc. (SWCC), headed by Elbert Bishop, to provide advice and counsel from the neighborhood level. Station-area task forces were organized at each proposed transit stop along the relocated Orange Line—including at the 5.6-acre vacant site known as Parcel 18. The Parcel 18 Task Force would become a key player in the parcel-to-parcel linkage plan.

In December 1975, representatives from the city, state, and neighborhoods traveled to Washington, D.C., to lobby Massachusetts Senator Edward W. Brooke and U.S. Secretary of Transportation William T. Coleman for federal funds to build the new, depressed Orange Line and the crosstown arterial street; to complete the South Cove Tunnel; and to begin the Roxbury replacement service. This visit would lead to a federal appropriation of nearly $500 million for these transportation projects—save the Roxbury replacement service. At the time, this was the largest public works project in the nation.

As the planning process was unfolding in the Southwest Corridor, and public investments began pouring in, the community started focusing on issues of desired uses and control of the planning and development process. Among the ideas put forward, in April 1977, the SWCC issued a report on "the Community Land Trust." Acknowledging that near each of the three transit stations—including at Parcel 18— commercial development would be strongly encouraged, the report advocated for the formation of such a public trust to better address real estate speculation, ownership, and control. In the Community Land Trust, the beneficiaries would be the residents of the surrounding community. Further, the trust would receive from the commonwealth of Massachusetts the land it currently held in the corridor and this land would be held in trust for the benefit of the community. Each development project would have terms setting "community benefit" requirements, i.e., the terms of the trust should require that certain direct benefits go to the community from each project proposed for a parcel of land. The report set the stage for discussions about a community trust, community benefits, and ownership and control, though the full outline of a community land trust as envisioned in the report was never fully realized.

By the late 1970s, the Parcel 18 Task Force had been organized and meeting weekly. As the most active station-area task force (SATF), the Parcel 18 group began a dialogue among its own members about ways to leverage this corridorwide redevelopment opportunity, starting with Parcel 18. They also started reaching out to the Asian American community through personal contacts and via the Chinatown/South Cove Neighborhood Council. Several members of the Parcel 18 Task Force were also members of the Minority Developers Association (MDA), which came into existence during the early 1980s. A viable core of minority developers had carved out a niche in the Boston market, albeit primarily in the minority neighborhoods of Roxbury, North Dorchester, and Mattapan. They had few opportunities to compete for projects outside the minority neighborhoods, but had to compete with white developers for projects within the minority community. For the most part, Boston's minority developers were excluded from the city's downtown market altogether.

By the mid-1980s, significant planning and development were underway in the Southwest Corridor. A new urban industrial park, which included Massachusetts computer giant Digital Equipment Corporation (DEC) as an anchor tenant, was slowly emerging in lower Roxbury. Bringing instant credibility to this community renewal effort, new residential units were coming on line, a master plan for the corridor had been approved, and banks began taking a second look at the area. The downtown Boston real estate market was booming as the Boston Redevelopment Authority (BRA) started juggling projects in the pipeline. It was within this context that the Parcel 18 Task Force proposed a plan to attempt to guide downtown prosperity to the Roxbury neighborhood—so as to try to accelerate the rebuilding process.

Three key ingredients of the plan as presented to the BRA by the Parcel 18 Task Force were as follows: economically connecting a downtown parcel of land with Parcel 18; providing a role for minority developers in this process, including with a major downtown project; and formulating a community benefits package predicated upon the success of the plan. Stephen Coyle, director of the BRA, endorsed the plan, as did Mayor Raymond Flynn and Governor Michael Dukakis. With their blessings, along with the BRA board's approval, the stage was set to implement the parcel-to-parcel linkage plan.

A downtown site was identified: the Kingston-Bedford multi-level parking garage adjacent to Chinatown in the financial district. A process was then put in place to select a minority development team via a request for qualifications (RFQ) to then be married to a national, "majority" developer through a request for proposal (RFP) process. The Parcel 18 Task Force and the Chinatown/South Cove Neighborhood Council remained at the center of this process with a review and approval role.

The Ruggles Street Station on the relocated Orange Line opened in 1987 at Parcel 18. The site became known as Ruggles Center. In March 1988, the BRA board tentatively designated a development team for the parcel-to-parcel linkage program—dubbed in BRA parlance as Project 1, Kingston/Bedford/Parcel 18. This team, Columbia Plaza Associates (CPA), was designated as a result of the RFQ process that engaged teams made up of leading minority real estate development professionals in the greater Boston area. The CPA team consisted of Ruggles-Bedford Associates, Inc., and the Chinatown Investment Group, Inc., along with four community development corporations. The Ruggles Center site adjacent to the Ruggles Street Station became a prime candidate for transit-oriented development.

To select a national developer as CPA's partner, an RFP process was put in motion. Metropolitan Structures was chosen via this mechanism to form the Metropolitan/Columbia Plaza Venture. The final designation of this team took place in February 1990. The community benefits package had been approved in June 1989 whereby 10 percent of the developers' fee, 10 percent of the net operating income, 10 percent of the net refinancing proceeds, and 10 percent of the net resale proceeds would flow into a community development fund, for each phase of the project.

The funds generated under this formula with respect to the Kingston-Bedford site, now known as One Lincoln Street, were to be distributed as follows: one-third for the benefit of the Chinatown community, one-third for the benefit of the Roxbury community, and one-third on a competitive basis for the benefit of communities throughout the city. The funds generated from Ruggles Center were to be distributed in the following manner: one-half for the benefit of the Chinatown community and one-half for the Roxbury community.

This was considered a watershed moment in Boston's real estate development history. Roxbury was poised to rise from the ashes of the aborted Southwest Expressway through the selection of a minority development team as a key player.

Given the downtown Boston real estate boom, it was anticipated that the One Lincoln Street project would be in the pipeline before Ruggles Center in Roxbury. However, the Boston downtown office market tanked soon after the relevant BRA accords were signed by the development team in the late 1980s. There was no demand for office space in downtown Boston. The focus then shifted to the Roxbury site at Ruggles Center. With the wrangling of BRA director Coyle, Mayor Flynn, and Governor Dukakis, the Massachusetts Water Resources Authority (MWRA) was tapped to become the anchor tenant at a newly constructed nine-story, 165,000-square-foot office building to be built as Phase I on this 5.6-acre site.

Peter Vanderwalker/Stull and Lee.

The MWRA and its predominantly white suburban workforce objected to relocating to this building in Roxbury. After it became clear that the MWRA would not move to Ruggles Center, attention turned to the Registry of Motor Vehicles (RMV), a state agency then located in cramped quarters near North Station. Again, there was serious objection by the RMV workforce to a Roxbury location, but the agency finally moved into the new office building at the Parcel 18 site. Then the building became a "sick" building and, after much drama, the RMV and its employees abandoned it, scattering to several different sites throughout Boston. This turn of events left the owners high and dry, paving the way for neighboring Northeastern University to step in and acquire the building for a bargain at auction and create Renaissance Park, which became office space for the University as well as the Whittier Street Neighborhood Health Center.

The Metropolitan/Columbia Plaza venture buckled under the pressure of this turn of events. The parcel-to-parcel linkage idea began to take on water along with this development partnership. As the downtown office market turned for the better, the One Lincoln Street site gained new life. However, Metropolitan Structures decided to withdraw from their partnership with Columbia

Plaza. John B. Hynes III, managing partner and principal with Gale and Wentworth, a national developer headquartered in Florham Park, New Jersey, carried both the local clout and national prominence to help create value at One Lincoln Street. This new partnership was approved by the BRA in February 2000 as the Kingston Bedford Joint Venture, LLC.

State Street Bank entered into a lease encompassing the largest amount of space in the history of downtown Boston with the owners of One Lincoln, thus creating the State Street Financial Center. The 36-story, 1.05 million-square-foot office and retail building was erected for $350 million, and was sold less than 18 months after completion for $671 per square foot— the highest price ever paid for commercial real estate in Boston. The 45 minority investors from the African American, Asian American, and Latino communities walked away with a substantial return on their investment. The four community development corporations realized upward of $1 million each. Roxbury and Chinatown community trusts received $15 million in community benefits, some of which was to be invested in affordable housing.

After fits and starts, the parcel-to-parcel linkage plan thus far has yielded a 36-story office tower in the financial district, a nine-story office building in Roxbury and a multilevel parking structure, nearly $20 million in community benefits, several new minority millionaires, a rejuvenated Roxbury, and a positive working relationship among three key racial and ethnic groups in a city still addressing its image problems.

Can this plan be duplicated elsewhere? On a recent ULI advisory services panel visit to Camden, New Jersey, such a plan was recommended among the development strategies to be used in the city's revitalization (see "Reviving Suburbia," page 54, January 2004). In Camden, the distressed Haddon Avenue is book ended by two thriving and expanding medical facilities, along with an emerging waterfront and downtown, where it is anticipated that over the next few years $450 million of new development will occur, 90 percent of which will be privately funded. (See "Panel Recommends Three Phases to Upgrade Camden's Haddon Avenue," page 137, June.) This follows on close to $400 million of mainly public investment in the Camden waterfront/downtown neighborhood. The question on the minds of many is: Can a waterfront/downtown parcel be economically connected to a parcel along needy Haddon Avenue?

Los Angeles may be another worthy candidate for such a plan. One possible contender for the downtown component of such a parcel-to-parcel linkage plan in L.A. could include the $1 billion commercial development around Staples Center to be developed by the Anschutz Entertainment Group (AEG). This complex will include hotels, theaters, restaurants, and stores across the street from the arena, replacing a string of parking lots that sit there now. A second possible L.A. candidate lies about a mile north of Staples Center, where onetime homebuilder Eli Broad, real estate executive James Thomas, and Los Angeles County's redevelopment agency have plans to build the Grand Avenue Project. This project will include $300 million in public parks and roadways, along with $900 million in residential and commercial properties. Neighborhood contenders for this plan could be drawn from several cash-needy projects in south L.A., east L.A., Chinatown, or Little Tokyo.

Similar to the Boston experience, it will take political and business will and motivation, along with patience and perseverance, to make such a plan a reality in other cities.

Philip S. Hart is president/CEO of Hart Realty Advisors, a division of Tanya Hart Communications, Inc., Hollywood, California. Over the past 30 years, Hart has been involved in the redevelopment of Boston's Southwest Corridor.

The third article is titled "Incubating Inner City Biotech" and appeared in the September 2006 issue of **Urban Land** magazine. In **New Orleans, Louisiana: A Strategy for Rebuilding**, again in the economic development and culture section of the report, one short-term action recommended under universities, health care, and medical services, is that:

> *"The combination of research universities, health centers, and the BioInnovation Center is evidence of the potential to develop an emerging biomedical sciences sector in New Orleans. This is an industry of the 21st century and—like many other cities with similar assets—New Orleans should determine whether it can indeed compete in this highly competitive sector, particularly as it emerges from the devastation caused by Katrina. Two factors working against New Orleans in the biosciences sector are the city's lack of a venture capital community attuned to this sector and a workforce lacking the skills and education that this industry requires."*

Incubating Inner-City Biotech

Philip S. Hart and William J. Gasper

As Los Angeles tries to develop a biomedical research campus in its inner-city area, it can look to a similar successful project in Boston for guidance.

Biotechnology, or biomedical research, stands to be one of the growth industries of the 21st century. Biotechnology fosters both the better understanding of biological mechanisms and the improvement and creation of products in a variety of sectors, such as agriculture, food processing, and pharmaceutics. Besides "classic" biotechnology—for example, baking bread and brewing beer with the help of yeast—there is also "modern" bio-

technology, principally based on the knowledge of gene function; genetically modified organisms (GMOs) are the products of this latest biotechnology. Biotechnology is a body of methods and techniques that employ as tools the living cells of organisms or parts or products of those cells (such as genes and enzymes).

Given the growth of this industry over the past 30 years in both the university and commercial sectors, related land use and development activity has been generated. The nature of this land use and development activity in relation to "modern" biotechnology has generally been centered around research universities, medical campuses, venture capital sources, public research funding, and a skilled workforce. Much of this activity has taken root in the Boston/Cambridge area, the San Francisco Bay Area, and San Diego, while more recently other municipalities have sought to become competitive in this arena.

Boston's Success

Biomedical research is not often associated with inner-city locations. However, in the Lower Roxbury and South End neighborhoods of Boston, a viable university and commercial biotechnology presence has been developing over the past 20 years. This "inner-city biotech" development is the focus of this article, which describes successes and lessons learned that can be applied to other inner-city locations interested in participating in this 21st-century industry.

Boston's inner-city biotech story began with the land clearance for the proposed Southwest Expressway right-of-way in 1966. In 1972, community pressure led to the cancellation of the Southwest Expressway, which opened up more than 200 acres (81 ha) for redevelopment in Boston's southwest corridor. By 1980, a new urban industrial park, CrossTown Industrial Park (CTIP), sited on 40 acres (16 ha) in Lower Roxbury, got its first tenant, Massachusetts computer giant Digital Equipment Corporation (DEC).

Meanwhile, during the early 1970s, in the South End neighborhood of Boston, adjacent to Lower Roxbury, the Boston University School of Medicine (BUSM) strategically solidified its relationships with its two neighboring hospitals, Boston City Hospital and University Hospital. Today, BU's schools of

medicine, dental medicine, and public health (collectively referred to as the Boston University Medical Campus or BU Medical) and Boston Medical Center (BMC)—the result of a merger of Boston City Hospital and University Hospital in July 1996—constitute a vibrant academic medical center with an inner-city community focus.

The Community Development Corporation of Boston, Inc., (CDCOB) was organized in 1969 as the economic development arm of the city of Boston Model Cities Program. Once the Model Cities demonstration period ended, CDCOB became an independent 501(c)(3) economic development organization that then turned its focus from making investments in local businesses to developing a long-range economic development strategy of creating an urban industrial park—CTIP—as a way to spur job creation and business development in the distressed Lower Roxbury neighborhood.

In 1984, CDCOB purchased a 50,000-square-foot (4,651-sq-m) paintbrush factory that occupied two industrial buildings just across the street from the DEC plant located at 801 Albany Street for a mere $60,000. Even with this modest purchase, CDCOB was unable to secure a conventional bank loan for this transaction as the city's downtown banks largely ignored Roxbury. Three years later, with the support of a U.S. Department of Commerce Economic Development Administration (EDA) Title IX grant, CDCOB began the shell and core renovation of the two factory buildings as speculative office and research and development space. BU took note of the activity at these vacant buildings a quarter-mile down the street from BUSM and, seeking to expand its biomedical research space for both BUSM research and educational programs and partnerships/incubation initiatives with biotech companies, partnered with CDCOB to plan and execute the development of an inner-city biotechnology facility at 801 Albany Street in Lower Roxbury's CrossTown Industrial Park.

CDCOB's agenda for 801 Albany Street was to continue bringing emerging technologies into this urban industrial park, so BU Medical's interest was timely. The building opened in 1989 as a biotechnology facility. In so doing, CDCOB and BU had to gain approval from the Boston Redevelopment Authority (BRA) to allow BU Medical to locate a facility on the Lower Roxbury side of Massachusetts Avenue from the South End prior to completing the medical campus master plan. BUSM occupied 90 percent of the structure on a long-term lease, which extends to 2014. CDCOB occupied the balance of the building with its corporate offices. From the beginning, BU's concept for this biotech facility was to provide a home for BUSM's Program in Biomedical Laboratory and Clinical Sciences, which prepares students for careers in biomedical technology; additional institutional research/clinical laboratories; and space to support joint venture relationships with biotech companies/commercial laboratories, including incubation of biotech startup companies.

BU's collaboration with CDCOB at 801 Albany Street was a harbinger of BU Medical's "near campus" development of biotech space. Soon after the opening of 801 Albany Street, BU commenced planning for a 35,000-square-foot (3,256-sq-m) biomedical research facility at 609 Albany Street (which opened in 1992) and joined with University Hospital (today, part of BMC) to develop city- and state-owned land at 650 to 700 Albany Street, which was being used for surface parking. These parking lots have since become BioSquare, Boston's only research park devoted exclusively to life sciences research and commercialization.

BioSquare covers 16 acres (6.5 ha) with a planned 2.5 million square feet (232,558 sq m) of laboratory, office, and support space, of which approximately 1.3 million gross square feet (120,930 sq m) have been developed to date, inclusive of three biomedical research buildings and two parking garages with a combined 2,400 parking spaces. The first of these buildings, the Center for Advanced Biomedical Research, opened in September 1993. In addition, construction began in March on the most recent BioSquare project, the $180 million, 192,000-square-foot (17,860-sq-m) National Emerging Infectious Diseases Laboratories. This project, where high containment level research will be conducted to develop diagnostics, vaccines, and treatments for dangerous infectious diseases, whether natural in origin or introduced through bioterrorism, is not without controversy. In early August, a Massachusetts state judge ruled that Boston University must file an updated environmental review. However, construction continues, and the university remains confident that the project will proceed as planned, with a 2008 opening.

Meanwhile, over the past 17 years, significant Boston University and biopharmaceutical company research activity has occurred at 801 Albany Street, much of which relates to diseases that afflict inner-city residents. For instance:

- During the early 1990s, BUSM Cancer Center researchers made important advances in the development of new therapies for the two most common genetic diseases in the world, sickle cell anemia and thalassemia.

- As of this writing, 801 is the headquarters for the Inner-City Asthma Study and the Inner-City Asthma Consortium, which are conducting investigations and clinical trials regarding interventions for asthma among inner-city children.

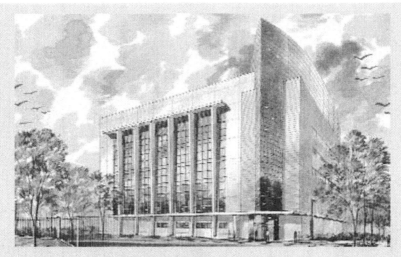

- School of Dental Medicine research faculty are conducting cutting-edge research on restorative dental materials.

- NitroMed, Inc., a publicly traded company, was a tenant at 801 in the mid-1990s, and developed and is marketing BiDil, a drug that treats congestive heart failure in African Americans.

- AdipoGenix, Inc., a startup biopharmaceutical company founded by BUSM faculty members and a current tenant at 801, is focused on the development of novel therapeutics for the treatment of disorders of fat tissue such as obesity and diabetes.

This biotech facility in Lower Roxbury has also met BU's objective of facilitating joint venture relationships with biotech companies and incubating biotech startup companies. In addition to the two companies mentioned above, CombinatoRx, Inc., a publicly traded company that identifies new disease targets and new medicines from combining already approved drugs, was incubated at 801 until it grew out of its space in 2001. In the meantime, the original 40-acre (16-ha) urban industrial park has grown to 75 acres (30 ha) and comprises office, industrial,

retail, public utility, and textile manufacturing uses; the DEC building and adjacent property have been replaced by Cross-Town Center, which includes Boston's first black-owned hotel, a parking structure, and two office buildings, with the first one now in construction with BU Medical as anchor tenant; and a planned 265-unit residential complex with first-floor retail space. Also, in contrast to 1984, when CDCOB could not secure a bank loan to purchase 801 Albany, banks are now very active in Lower Roxbury and its surrounding neighborhoods.

Los Angeles Moves Forward

In Los Angeles, plans are gaining momentum for the development of an Urban BioMed Research Park sited in the distressed East Los Angeles neighborhood near the County-USC (University of Southern California) Hospital. The USC Health Sciences Campus is a major medical campus in East Los Angeles, encompassing Norris Cancer Center, USC/LA Hospital, Doheny Eye

Center, USC Medical School, and other university-affiliated centers. The proposed BioMed Research Park would cover more than 1.6 million square feet (148,837 sq m) of space and is to be built in phases over a period of ten or more years. USC is slated to be the major anchor tenant, with current construction plans totaling 585,000 square feet (54,418 sq m) in the first five years of the phased development process. USC's commitment to the project has been demonstrated thus far with extensive investment in site preparation, infrastructure, and new medical research facilities.

This East L.A. neighborhood is predominantly Latino; Roxbury is mostly African American. Both of these inner-city neighborhoods, which are 3,000 miles (4,830 km) apart, have public housing and jail facilities within a short distance from major medical facilities governed by important private research universities. The East L.A. site under consideration for this Urban BioMed Research Park comprises over 1,000 acres (404 ha) and its development is to be governed by a city of Los Angeles and Los Angeles County Joint Powers Authority. The first phase of the USC portion of this public/private biomed research park is to be built on a 40-acre (16-ha) site and is to be a stem-cell research center supported by renowned business leader and philanthropist Eli Broad.

Compared with the Boston/Cambridge area's biomedical industry, Los Angeles's is relatively young, with more than half its companies having started during the last 15 years. Despite the youth of the industry in southern California, its future there is bright, as numerous economists and political leaders see biotechnology as a key growth engine for the 21st century. With a recent $3 billion stem-cell ballot initiative approved by the voters in November 2004, the state of California has become one of the strongest supporters of the biosciences industry in general and stem-cell research in particular. It is expected that Los Angeles's biomed industry as a whole will benefit from this initiative.

Indeed, Los Angeles already has a large base of biomedical research activity, including its universities as well as private research institutions. Thousand Oaks, California—based Amgen—the largest U.S. biotech firm, with over 7,000 employees worldwide and $3 billion in annual revenues—is the cornerstone of the commercial biotechnology industry in the L.A. area. (Amgen opened its first Massachusetts research facility at BioSquare in 2000, taking advantage of BioSquare's facilities, collaborative environment, and access to biomedical support services, until it moved to an Amgen-owned facility a few miles away.)

Southern California has a number of other major manufacturers of pharmaceuticals and medical devices, but it has not produced other strong biotech companies. The metropolitan Los Angeles area falls well behind the San Francisco Bay Area and the San Diego area in venture capital, initial public offerings, and fast-growing biotechnology companies. Similarly, Los Angeles lags well behind Boston/Cambridge on these same measures.

With both the more mature inner-city biotechnology activities in Boston as with the embryonic work in L.A., private research universities with medical centers are at the root of this effort. Given the location of this university medical presence in two needy urban neighborhoods—Lower Roxbury and East Los Angeles—it is critically important for each university to provide local residents with the education necessary to move into the biotech industry. This is why the BU program in Biomedical Laboratory and Clinical Sciences, which has been located at 801 Albany Street from the very beginning, bears replication in the L.A. Urban BioMed Research Park. Indeed, this program has brought much recognition over the years to Boston University and to 801 Albany, as a result of CityLab and CityLab Academy, two highly successful educational programs.

CityLab is a biotechnology learning laboratory that provides access to state-of-the-art laboratory facilities and curriculum in biotechnology for middle and high school teachers and students. With support from federal and private funding agencies, tens of thousands of students and teachers have attended workshops held at 801. The ten-year-old CityLab Academy, based at 801 Albany Street, is a nine-month biotechnology skills training and education program designed for economically and academically disadvantaged students. It is offered on a full scholarship basis for eligible high school graduates interested in pursuing a career and further education in biotechnology. Upon successful completion, graduates are provided with assistance in securing entry-level biotechnology jobs.

Lessons Learned

What lessons can be learned from the inner-city biotech success story in Boston that can be applied to Los Angeles and other municipalities interested in attracting and/or developing this 21st century industry? These lessons include the following:

- Vision. In Boston, the visionaries included Boston University and the Community Development Corporation of Boston.

- Location, Location, Location. Normally, suburban locations are regarded as more ideal sites for biotechnology development. Boston and now Los Angeles are angling to tell another story about ideal locations for such activity.

- Be Flexible. Be prepared to change direction if the initial plan is not working.

- Collaborate. Work with and not against federal, state, and local officials and agencies, as well as the local community; view them as partners. This lesson is going to be particularly important in East Los Angeles as USC, the city of Los Angeles, and the county of Los Angeles endeavor to jointly plan and develop a major urban biomed research park in a challenged neighborhood.

- Be Reasonable. Be reasonable and fair, particularly in negotiating financial terms with partners, tenants, contractors, consultants, etc.

- Communicate Well. Poor communication will bring confusion into every phase of the project.

- Know Your Customers. Understand the needs and desires of your tenants/occupants and do your best to satisfy them. This includes your university researchers doing sponsored research as well as the commercial biotech and commercial laboratory tenants.

- Be Patient. Remember—it is a marathon and not a sprint to the finish line.

Philip S. Hart is president/CEO of Hart Realty Advisors, based in Hollywood, California.

William J. Gasper is associate vice president for financial and business affairs at Boston University Medical Campus. Hart and Gasper began working together nearly 20 years ago to help create inner-city biotech activities in Boston.

Reprinted with permission of ULI-Urban Land Institute, Washington, DC.

Bio medical miracles

A biomedical park is a laboratory containing a community
Such as USC adjacent East LA or BU adjacent Roxbury
Like any large scientific experiment it is laid down on synergy
Of theoretical principles applied and documented in a history

Think of the laboratory in a tent set up on three poles
Pole one location by a research university
based upon the primary real estate location vector
that proximity to like industry brings growth of a sector.
Pole two for jumping out of incubators
Medical entrepreneurs bend the pole to propel over the bar
carrying innovations on shoulders making new product stars.
Pole three magnetic pole of community conductivity
pulls the bodies of students and lab assistants living in the vicinity
thru flaps in the tent to a future life of productivity.

All theses forces brought a victory to Roxbury's urban core
By extending science in an area institutions left unexplored
But it can happen anywhere, and there's one idea more:
You might be surprised that this tent of social enterprise
lies on a ground cloth of tax credit magic carpet support
which raises the short term measured financial return
To match the long term benefits that society will earn.

"Incubating Inner City Biotech" is a case study of a success story in developing a biomedical sector in the predominantly African American Roxbury neighborhood in Roxbury—my former neighborhood—and its applicability to developing an Urban BioMed Research Park in the predominantly Latino East Los Angeles neighborhood. This case study is equally relevant to New Orleans.

Both of these Boston, Massachusetts case study articles also describe the rigors of redevelopment after a man-made disaster, that of razing over 200 acres in anticipation of building an expressway. Once this ill-fated exercise in urban planning was scrapped, there was a need to redevelop these 200 plus acres in a predominantly African American community. This mixed-use redevelopment is well on its way to completion some forty years after it was razed. Ideally it will not take forty years from August 29, 2005 to rebuild the new New Orleans, though federal recovery czar Donald Powell estimates it will take 25 years. Perhaps a worthy goal is to do as the ULI Expert Team and Advisory Team did and target the 300th anniversary of the founding of New Orleans—or 2018— as the year in which the new New Orleans will be in its full and sustainable bloom. The three case studies included in this concluding section of my book represent work I have been actively involved with since the early 1970s to redevelop urban centers in post-disaster situations. It is this expertise that I brought to New Orleans in November 2005 with the view of assisting this distressed city along with my Urban Land Institute colleagues, and I remain convinced we did a fine job and that our work will indeed be the blueprint to ReNew Orleans.

The efficacy of the ULI report in November 2005 is recently borne out by recommendations for rebuilding made by Ed Blakely. In a March 30, 2007 New Orleans Times Picayune article, Blakely is quoted as saying he wants to put $1.1 billion toward revitalizing isolated pockets of the city—from high traffic Canal Street to the hard hit Lower Ninth Ward. Blakeley's announcement of seventeen target zones—intended to be the focus for development incentives—comes as a part of what Mayor Nagin called 'phase one' of what, so far, has been a sluggish recovery.

Blakely goes on to note that the majority of the resources are going to be spent citywide—about 60 percent. The other 40 percent are going to these 17 areas in phase one. The zones in the city are divided into three categories: rebuild, redevelop or renew. Each development zone is approximately one-half mile in diameter, although the area can vary slightly.

Listed as rebuild zones are the Holy Cross neighborhood in the Lower Ninth Ward and the neighborhood near the old Lake Forest Plaza in New Orleans East. Among the redevelop zones are Carrollton Avenue at Interstate 10, Harrison Avenue from Canal Boulevard to City Park Avenue, and four other neighborhood, among the renew zones are Canal Street through downtown, Freret Street and the Farmers Market in Uptown, along with seven other zones.

This phased zone strategy creates the opportunity to create the kind of clustering around civic assets—building around these places so that we can make this a stronger city in the end, noted Blakely. Mayor Nagin said the city has had difficulty in the past seeing big projects through to completion and that the reality is that the rebuilding will be a 10-year cycle and that 17 target areas is about what the city can handle at one time.

The target areas which Blakely said are in line with citizen recommendations, are set to be part of a broader redevelopment plan expected to include economic initiatives and city-wide improvements, such as stepped-up enforcement of blighted properties.

The target areas are set to be taken to the Louisiana Recovery Authority for federal money. This phased, zone approach with 17 target areas is a cluster strategy for redevelopment that mirrors what would be expected to result from the ULI's strategies for rebuilding New Orleans. The unfortunate thing is that for a variety of reasons it has taken so long to reach this point. African Americans have been an important component of New Orleans in both an historic and current context. It is vitally important that African Americans and the future of New Orleans be wedded as well.

As reported in the *New York Times*, April 10, 2007, 14 of the 17 areas Blakely has singled out as part of this phased investment strategy are in the more promising, less flooded western part of the city. A combination of incentives for developers and public infrastructure spending will be used to rebuild these areas, according to Blakely. *The New York Times* article goes on to note that awareness of racial and economic realities is reflected in Blakely's relatively modest plan; it is not an effort to make over the entire city all at once. Instead, the plan revolves around localized attention to promising zones that, if they take off, could have a transforming effect on the whole. Blakely's take on his plan is that if he can pump life in these places, it may be possible to pump life back into the entire city.

The picture in its entirety is too daunting to be tackled completely, which follows the logic of ULI's strategies for rebuilding New Orleans first offered in November 2005. A second entrenched hurdle for Blakely and the city, according to the *New York Times*, is the paperthin economy. Again, ULI addressed this issue in its economic development strategies put forth over one year and a half ago. As the *Times* article goes on to note, if the city's paperthin economy is not built up—essentially created wholesale, most promisingly on hopes of redeveloping a downtown medical and bioscience complex here—all of Blakely's exercises could be for naught.

The story of the recovery of the city of New Orleans is going to be a longrunning saga. I plan to revisit this topic in another 3-5 years to assess where the recovery efforts stand at that point. In addition, I plan to continue my role as a participant-observer in the process— writing about the recovery when the opportunity presents itself — as well as working to bring financial and development resources to the city where appropriate. I truly hope that when I update this book in about five years that the story I tell is a more positive and uplifting tale.

Epilogue

Ultimately, the continuing tragedy in New Orleans is a story about people. Whether, George Bush and his view of the role of government in a post-Reagan minimalist perspective or Ray Nagin who is still struggling to govern in an apocalyptic scenario while still undergoing on-the-job- training, it is people who are at the center of the story and the storm.

Social psychology is the study of the individual in society. How does the individual find their voice within a larger, often bureau-cratic social structure is a key question in this particular realm of the social sciences. To a certain extent, individuals can rely upon their own devices to survive and thrive in society. Yet, at the same time there is a need for collective action in order for the social contract to be the compass for the public good.

In considering New Orleans, post-Katrina, there is a need for indi-vidual action that is working in concert with collective action. To date, such a concerto has not been played out. At the individual level, there are stories such as the white musician I met while in New Orleans in November 2005 who lost his home in Lakeview to flooding, and in the process lost all of his equipment and sheet music. He recently became a proud homeowner in this middle class neighborhood on Lake Pontchartrain after moving from a walk up apartment with his young family in the French Quarter. He seemed to be quite a determined individual—yet he was looking for some assistance that could only come from a collective source.

Or there is that young African American male I referred to earlier in this account who was evidently contemplating suicide at the Sheraton New Orleans Hotel in November 2005. Whatever demons were tugging at his heart that night had overwhelmed his individual spirit—he too was looking for some collective help that is part of the social contract.

Recently I re-connected with my friend Jim Blackwell. He and his wife Myrt live in an eastern suburb toward Slidell. He and his wife self-evacuated two days before Katrina hit the city. Initially they re-located to Texarkana, Texas. They were out of their home in a middle class area from August 27, 2005 until the first of July in 2006. The Blackwells live in a two story home in which the first floor had been destroyed by flooding. Jim told me that in their immediate neighborhood there are 210 homes. Of this number he reported that 86 homeowners had returned by late January 2007 and were working on repairing their homes. He told me another 81 homeowners indicated they planned to return but had not yet done so. He did not know about the balance of the homeowners among this group of 210 homes. So, after more than 18 months after Katrina in this middle class enclave, just over one third of the homeowners had returned. Like Jim and Myrt, they were able to muster the resources to reclaim their homes. In Jim's instance, the same contractor who initially built his home was doing the renovation work on the first floor, so he was fairly confident that the quality of work would be satisfactory. I was so pleased when I called the Blackwells in New Orleans and Myrt answered and told me they were okay and back at home.

I also remember meeting nearly 300 people at the Dream Center in Los Angeles in September 2005 who had been displaced from New Orleans with Katrina and the subsequent flooding. The Sunday before this meeting Bishop Blake had requested an offering at services that morning to assist victims of the storm. We raised nearly $50,000 that Sunday for this purpose. The following Friday Bishop Blake was taking $25,000 of this offering to the Dream

Center where these families and individuals had been evacuated. I was asked to attend with the Bishop, along with actress Victoria Rowell and actor Courtney B. Vance. We were scheduled to meet at the Dream Center at 10am. I attended an Urban Land Institute Los Angeles Executive Committee meeting early that morning before heading over to the Dream Center. At that meeting we were informed that ULI would be getting involved in a major way in New Orleans and the Gulf Coast.

When I arrived at the Dream Center at about 9:30am people were everywhere, including the press. I eventually located Bishop's son Larry, who is his chief aide, and was told where to gather. We then proceeded to gather around 10am in a gymnasium where we were surrounded by Katrina evacuees of all ages looking confused and bewildered. As the press gathered as well, Bishop began by leading us in prayer. He then made a statement, followed by me, then Victoria, then Courtney. Larry then handed Bishop a large envelope filled with money, which Bishop then began handing out to those Gulf Coast evacuees there before him. It was like a scene from the Bible—Bishop was a savior of sorts with his disciples by his side, and all these hungry souls receiving this manna from heaven. Unlike biblical times perhaps, the press was pressed together covering this event.

Afterwards, I stuck around talking to as many evacuees as possible. In addition, many approached us to ask questions. In my brief remarks to the press after Bishop had addressed them, I had said that ULI plans to play a role in New Orleans and the Gulf Coast to do what it can as a land use organization to help rebirth, renew and rebuild. ULI has kept its word, now it is up to the powers that be to keep their word.

References

American Institute of Architects. *The Economic and Construction Outlook in the Gulf States after Hurricane Katrina.* October 2005.

Blackwell, James E. and Hart, Philip S. *Cities, Suburbs and Blacks: A Study of Concerns, Distrust and Alienation.* New York, General Hall, 1982.

Blackwell, James E. and Hart, Philip S. *Race Relations in Boston: Institutional Neglect, Turmoil and Change.* The Boston Committee, Boston, MA. 1983.

Burdeau, Cain. "9th Ward can be rebuilt, planners say," Associated Press, Jan. 7, 2007.

City of New Orleans, City Planning Commission. *New Orleans Land Use Plan,* 1999.

Duncan, Jeff. "Dome Series," *New Orleans Times Picayune,* August 27 – August 30, 2006.

Dyson, Michael Eric. *Come Hell or High Water: Hurricane Katrina and the Color of Disaster.* New York: Basic Civitas Books, 2006.

Guillermo's Notes. Urban Land Institute Meeting, Sheraton Hotel, New Orleans, Louisiana, November 18, 2005.

Haley, Alex. *Roots: The Saga of an American Family.* New York: Doubleday. 1976.

Hart, Tanya, Whitmore-Guscott, Valerie, Hart, *Philip S. Dark Passages,* BET, 1990. A documentary film.

Horne, Jed. *Breach of Faith: Hurricane Katrina and the Near Death of A Great American City.* New York, Random House, 2006.

Kabacoff, Pres. "Operation Rebirth," *Urban Land,* Washington, D.C., January 2006.

Kenny, Kath. "Sydney Professor to head New Orleans recovery," The University of Sydney, Australia, December 12, 2006.

Kreisler, Barbara. "A Rude Awakening," *Urban Land,* Washington, D.C., January 2006.

Landrieu, Mitchell J. "Higher Common Ground: There but for the Grace of God go I." State of Louisiana, Office of the Lieutenant Governor, November 29, 2005.

Landrieu, Mitchell J. Speech given at the Louisiana Recovery and Rebuilding Conference presented by The American Institute of Architects, undated.

Landrieu, Mitchell J. and Davis, Angele. "New Orleans, Louisiana Rebirth: Restoring the Soul of America," undated.

Lee, Spike. *When the Levees Broke*, HBO, 2006. An HBO Documentary Film Event.

Levy, Clifford J. "New Orleans is Not Ready to Think Small, or Even Medium." *New York Times*, December 11, 2005.

Louisiana Economic Development. Katrina Community Revitalization Act of 2005: Proposed Federal Business Tax Legislation Relief, Draft, September 19, 2005.

Los Angeles Times. "Real Estate: Investment firm buys New Orleans high-rise," December 28, 2006.

Los Angeles Times. "The Worst of 2006/Architecture," Christopher Hawthorne, December 17, 2006.

Merton, Robert K. "Discrimination and the American Creed," in Robert M. McIver (ed.), *Discrimination and National Welfare*. New York. Institute for Religious and Social Studies, 1949.

Murphy, Thomas. "A Call for Action in New Orleans." *Urban Land*, Washington, D.C., January 2006.

Muro, Mark and Katz, Bruce. "Raising the Roof in New Orleans." *Urban Land*, Washington, D.C., January 2006.

Myrdal, Gunnar. *An American Dilemma: The Negro Problem and Modern Democracy*. New York: Harper & Brothers, 1944.

National Public Radio. Interview: Jed Horne, author of Breach of Faith and of the *New Orleans Times Picayune,* discusses New Orleans and Hurricane Katrina, July 11, 2006.

Nyren, Ron. "Visions for New Orleans." *Urban Land*, Washington, D.C., January 2006.

Olson, Jr., Mancur. *The Logic of Collective Action: Public Goods and the Theory of Goods.* New York: Schocken Books, 1968.

Pascal, Anthony H. *Racial Discrimination in Economic Life*. Lexington, MA. D. C. Heath, 1972.

Real Property Law Reporter. Repenos v. U.S.: Wading Through the Swamp of Federal Regulations of Wetlands, by Judy V. Davidoff, Timothy D. Cremin, and Elizabeth N. Sibbett, November 2006.

Regional Planning Commission. Comprehensive Economic Development Strategy (CEDS), October 2000.

Rosan, Richard M. "The Path to Rebuilding." *Urban Land*, Washington, D.C., September 2006.

Ryan, Timothy P. The Economic Impact of the Louis Armstrong International Airport, May 2004.

Sack, Kevin and Simmons, Ann. "Memorics fill the void on a block in New Orleans," *Los Angeles Times*, December 25, 2006.

Schambach, R.W. *The Power Book: Power Promises for Victorious Living*. Harrison House, Dallas, TX, 1953.

Simmons, Ann M. The master of post-disaster, Los Angeles Times, December 20, 2006.

Simmons, Ann M. "Week of homicides racks New Orleans," *Los Angeles Times*, January 7, 2007.

Smiley, Tavis (Editor). *The Covenant*. Third World Press, Chicago, 2006.

Sower, Christopher and Miller, Paul A. *The Changing Power Structure in Agriculture: An Analysis of Negative Versus Positive Organization Power*, reprint from Our Changing Rural Society: Perspectives and Trends, James H. Copp, Editor, Iowa State University Press, Ames, Iowa, 1964.

Steele, Shelby. *White Guilt*. New York: Harper Collins, 2006.

Taimerica Management Company. Draft: Katrina Economic Impact, October 1, 2005.

Taylor, Marilyn J. "Accommodating Need, Preparing for Growth," *Urban Land*, Washington, D.C., January 2006.

The Brookings Institution Metropolitan Policy Program. New Orleans After the Storm: Lessons from the Past, a Plan for the Future, October 2005.

The Planning Report. Ed Blakely to Head Recovery Efforts in New Orleans, Volume XX, No. 2, Dec./Jan. 2006-07.

Thurow, Lester. *Poverty and Discrimination*. Washington, D.C. Brookings Institute, 1967.

Urban Land Institute. A Strategy for Hollywood's Comeback. An Advisory Services Report, Washington, D.C., March 11-16, 2001.

Urban Land Institute. Camden, New Jersey. An Advisory Services Report, Washington, D.C. June 6-11, 2004.

Urban Land Institute. St. Paul Gateway District, San Antonio, Texas. An Advisory Services Report, Washington, D.C. November 14-19, 2004.

Urban Land Institute. New Orleans, Louisiana: A Strategy for Rebuilding. An Advisory Services Report. November 12-18, 2005.

Urban Land Institute. Great Streets, Washington, D.C. An Advisory Services Program Report. January 17-20, 2006.

Urban Land Institute. One ULI. Supplement to Urban Land, 2006.

Varney, James. Nagin backpedals, apologizes. January 18, 2006, *New Orleans Times Picayune*.

Vartabedian, Ralph. New Orleans levee-risk study faulted, *Los Angeles Times*, December 31, 2006.

Vogel, Mary. "Moving Toward High-Performance Infrastructure." *Urban Land*. October 2006.

Whitlock, Warren. Rebuilding the Soul of New Orleans. *Urban Land*. Washington, D.C., January 2006.

Williams, Carol J. Hurricane center chief issues final warning. *Los Angeles Times*, January 3, 2007.

Wilson, William Julius. The Declining Significance of Race. Chicago, Illinois. University of Chicago Press. 1978.

Whoriskey, Peter. New Orleans Repeats Mistakes as it Rebounds: Many Houses Built in Areas Katrina Flooded Are Not on Raised Foundations. The Washington Post, January 4, 2007.

Zell, Jennifer. "Visions of Green." *Urban Land*. Washington, D.C., October 2006.

About the Author

Philip Hart is Executive Director of the Urban Land Institute Los Angeles (ULI LA) District Council. ULI LA was the first of the 62 ULI District Councils in the United States, Europe and Asia to reach 2,000 members. Hart also owns two small businesses located in Hollywood, CA., one a real estate development company and the other an entertainment company. Hart has been a ULI member for over 20 years, initially joining when he lived in Boston, MA. With ULI LA, Hart has been active with the Executive Committee, the Program Committee, and the Inner City Policy Committee, which organizes the annual Urban Marketplace.

Hart took early retirement as Professor of Sociology and Director of the William Monroe Trotter Institute at the University of Massachusetts, Boston, in 2002, after over 25 years with the University. While at UMass, Boston, Hart was also a Senior Fellow with the John W. McCormack Institute of Public Affairs for three years. On two separate occasions Hart was a Visiting Research Sociologist at UCLA's Ralph Bunche Center for African American Studies.

Hart has served on several ULI advisory services panels, including in New Orleans in 2005 after Hurricane Katrina. The ULI report, "New Orleans, Louisiana: A Strategy for Rebuilding" is helping guide the redevelopment of this devastated city. In early 2006, Hart served on a ULI panel in Washington, D.C. assisting that city with its $100 million, 4-year 'Great Streets' initiative. Hart has also co-sponsored ULI advisory services panels, including a 2001 visit to Hollywood, CA. That ULI report "A Strategy for Hollywood's Comeback" has been guiding redevelopment of this iconic neighborhood.

Hart has a 25+ year history as a real estate developer. He is master developer of CrossTown Industrial Park (CTIP) in Boston's Roxbury neighborhood. This 75-acre urban business park that opened in 1980 has high tech, biotech, university, office, retail, industrial, textile manufacturing, hotel, public utility and residential tenants. Hart was project manager for the $60 million, 5,000-seat West Angeles Cathedral in South Los Angeles, which was dedicated in April 2001. Hart is Senior Advisor for the West Angeles Building Strategy Team for the West Angeles Campus and West Angeles Village developments. Hart is part of a team involved with Brownfields Remediation and Development in Carson, CA.

Hart has also been active with issues of urban mass transit in both Boston and Los Angeles. In Boston he directed the Southwest Corridor Special Mobility Study in the early 1970s, an origin-destination study that was an element in the regional Boston Transportation Planning Review (BTPR) that led to the relocation of the MBTA Orange Line, the creation of the MBTA Silver Line, and the creation of a new crosstown arterial, Melnea Cass Boulevard. In Los Angeles, Hart was active with the Hollywood Chamber of Commerce in support of the MTA Red Line and currently serves on the MTA Expo Line Construction Authority Urban Design Committee. Phase 1 of the MTA Expo Line to run from downtown LA to Culver City is funded at $640 million and is scheduled to open in 2010. Phase 2 of the MTA Expo Line will run from Culver City to Santa Monica and is not yet funded.

Hart has published widely on a variety of topics over the past 25 years, including:

- **African Americans and the Future of New Orleans: Rebirth, Renewal and Rebuilding – An American Dilemma**, Amber

Books, Phoenix and New York, book manuscript to be published in May 2007.

- "A Time to Build in the City of Angels," a book chapter on community development ministries of West Angeles Church of God in Christ and First AME Church in Los Angeles, in the anthology **In the Vineyards: Churches and Community Development,** manuscript to be published in 2007.

- "Minority Developers and New Orleans," **Urban Land,** October 2006.

- "Incubating Inner City Biotech," **Urban Land**, September 2006.

- "Hollywood's Time to Shine," **Urban Land**, September 2005.

- "Boston's Parcel to Parcel Linkage Plan," **Urban Land,** July 2005.

- **Bessie Coleman: Just the Facts,** Lerner Publishing, Minneapolis, MN, 2005. A book for middle school and high school ages.

- Technology as an Economic Catalyst in Rural and Depressed Places in Massachusetts, research monograph for University of Massachusetts under contract with U.S. Department of Commerce, 2000.

- **Up in the Air: The Story of Bessie Coleman,** Carolrhoda Books, Minneapolis, MN, 1996. For 8-13 year old readers.

- "The Competitive Advantage of the Inner City: Race Matters?" Occasional Paper, William Monroe Trotter Institute, University of Massachusetts, Boston, 1995.

- **Flying Free: America's First Black Aviators,** Lerner Publishing Company, Minneapolis, MN, 1992. For 10-15 year old readers.

- "Institutional Effectiveness in the Production of Black Bac-calaureates," in **In Pursuit of Inequality in Higher Education**, General Hall Books, New York, New York, 1987.

- Institutional Effectiveness in the Production of Black Bacca-laureates, Southern Education Foundation, Atlanta, GA., 1984.

- **Cities, Suburbs and Blacks: A Study of Concerns, Distrust and Alienation** (with James E. Blackwell), General Hall Books, New York, New York, 1982.

- Hart is listed in **Black Authors and Illustrators of Children's Books**, the 2006, 2000, and 1996 editions.

- Hart is listed in the 2007 edition of **Something About the Author** a reference series that publishes the lives and works of authors and illustrators of children's books.

Hart has also produced documentary films and syndicated radio programming for nearly 25 years. Hart's documentary films "Flyers In Search of A Dream" and "Dark Passages" have been best-sellers in the PBS Video catalogue for over a decade. "Flyers" tells the story of America's first black aviators. "Dark Passages" tells the story of the Atlantic slave trade and was shot on location in West Africa. Hart has been writer, producer for syndicated radio programs 'Hart Moments,' 'Hollywood Live with Tanya Hart,' and 'Ray Charles: The Music Lives On'. Hart's entertainment company currently has several television and feature film projects in various stages of development.

Hart is active in civic affairs both in Los Angeles and Boston. In Los Angeles, Hart is; Chair of Ability First's Housing Development Task Force which builds non-HUD financed accessible, affordable housing in Southern California; Vice Chair of Ability First's Housing Governance Board which has built over 300 HUD-financed acces-sible, affordable apartments throughout Southern California; member of the Board of Managers of the Hollywood Wilshire

YMCA; Chair of the West Angeles Church of God in Christ planned giving program, Kingdom Builders; member of the Rotary Club of Los Angeles where he serves on the Rotary Cares Committee which is assisting the American Cancer Society in its capital campaign to build a Hope Lodge in Los Angeles and on the Scholarship Committee; member of the Hollywood Chamber of Commerce where he serves on the Economic Development Committee; a member of the Los Feliz Homeowners Association and the Los Feliz Improvement Association. Hart recently was asked to join the Board of Governors of the Los Angeles County Economic Development Corporation (LAEDC). Hart also serves on the Mayor's Economy and Jobs Task Force in Los Angeles and the City of LA Planning Department Historic Resources Survey Advisory Committee.

Hart is a native of Denver, Colorado. He was educated in the Denver Public Schools. He earned his B.A. degree in sociology from the University of Colorado, Boulder, where he was a cum laude graduate as well as a student-athlete. He was inducted into the University's Distinguished Alumni Gallery in 1995. Hart's masters and doctorate degrees in sociology were earned at Michigan State University.

Hart lives in Los Angeles, California and in Edgartown, MA on the island of Martha's Vineyard.

ORDER FORM

WWW.AMBERBOOKS.COM
African-American Self Help and Career Books

Fax Orders: 480-283-0991

Telephone Orders: 480-460-1660

Online Orders: E-mail: Amberbks@aol.com

Postal Orders: Send Checks & Money Orders to:

Amber Books Publishing

1334 E. Chandler Blvd., Suite 5-D67, Phoenix, AZ 85048

_____ *African Americans and the Future of New Orleans* $15.95

_____ *The African-American Family's Guide to Tracing Our Roots* $14.95

_____ *Literary Divas: The Top 100+ Most Admired African American Women in Literature* $16.95

_____ *Beside Every Great Man…Is A Great Woman* $14.95

_____ *How to Be an Entrepreneur and Keep Your Sanity* $14.95

_____ *Real Estate and Wealth…Investing in the American Dream* $16.95

_____ *African American Real Estate Guide—$30,000 in 30 Days,* $14.95

_____ *The African-American Writer's Guide to Successful Self-Publishing* $14.95

_____ *Fighting for Your Life: The African American Criminal Justice System Survival Guide* $14.95

_____ *Urban Suicide: The Enemy We Choose Not to See* $14.95

_____ *How to Get Rich When You Ain't Got Nothing* $14.95

_____ *The African-American Job Seeker's Guide to Successful Employment* $14.95

_____ *The African-American Teenagers Guide to Personal Growth, Health, Safety, Sex and Survival* $19.95

_____ *No Mistakes: The African-American Teen Guide to Growing Up Strong* $14.95

_____ *Black Out: The Black Person's Guide to Redefining A Career Path Outside of Corporate America* $15.95

_____ *2007-2009 African American Scholarship Guide for Students and Parents* $16.95

Name:_____

Company Name:_____

Address: _____

City:_____State:_____Zip:_____

Telephone: (_____) _____E-mail:_____

Future of New Orleans	$15.95	❏ Check ❏ Money Order ❏ Cashiers Check
Tracing Our Roots	$14.95	❏ Credit Card: ❏ MC ❏ Visa ❏ Amex ❏ Discover
Literary Divas	$16.95	
Beside Every Great Man	$14.95	CC#_____
How to be an Entrepreneur	$14.95	
Real Estate and Wealth	$15.95	Expiration Date:_____
Successful Self-Publishing	$14.95	
Fighting for Your Life	$14.95	**Payable to:** Amber Books
Urban Suicide	$14.95	1334 E. Chandler Blvd., Suite 5-D67
How to Get Rich	$14.95	Phoenix, AZ 85048
Job Seeker's Guide	$14.95	
Teenagers Guide	$19.95	**Shipping:** $5.00 per book. Allow 7 days for delivery.
No Mistakes	$14.95	**Sales Tax:** Add 7.05% to books shipped to AZ addresses.
Black Out	$15.95	**Total enclosed: $**_____
Scholarship Guide	$15.95	